THE TECH ACADEMY

LEARNCODINGANYWHERE.COM

Introduction to Coding in Hours With Python

LEVEL 1

A Guide to Programming for Students With No Prior Experience

Written by:

Jack C. Stanley and Erik D. Gross,
Co-Founders of The Tech Academy

TABLE OF CONTENTS

TABLE OF CONTENTS

TABLE OF CONTENTS

TABLE OF CONTENTS

INTRODUCTION

Welcome to the first book in our series of introductory Python texts!

We (Jack and Erik) took it upon ourselves to write this book in a way that is understandable to non-technical individuals and we wanted to create a resource for those who have never written code before. Many introductory programming books out there assume too much prior knowledge on the part of the reader. We instead attempted to write in a way that our non-tech savvy friends, family and associates could comprehend and follow. As an example of this, one of our benchmarks in developing chapters and assignments was: "Could our parents do this?"

The two primary barriers to entry into the tech industry are:

1. The massive required technical vocabulary of over 1,000 terms (which some people spew out with no concern for their audience), and

2. The tendency of some experts to talk down to beginners or the "uninitiated" in a way that belittles their knowledge level and is over their heads. A sort of clique mentality can form with experienced programmers that acts as a buffer against new entries to the team.

So, this book stands as a rebellion against "business as usual" – we instead assume no prior technical knowledge on the part of the reader, and we will explain and define every technical term and concept in plain English.

It is notable that the logo of our school (The Tech Academy) contains a bridge. This bridge not only pays homage to the city we are headquartered in (Portland, Oregon – which is sometimes referred to as "Bridge City" or "Bridgetown"), it represents a passage of the gap between general society and technically-trained individuals. The Tech Academy bridge is a path that leads to an understanding of technology and competence in coding.

Instead of throwing you right into writing code, we are going to lay a foundation for you to build upon by breaking down fundamental terms and concepts that will open the door for an understanding of the actions you will take into this book. Or put another way, instead of turning you into a "coding parrot" who simply types what we tell them to, we are going to prepare you to actually comprehend what you are doing as you do. Therefore, you will not write any code until the second chapter of this book.

So, without further ado, let's dive in and start with the fundamentals, including what terms like *program* and *code* really mean.

CHAPTER 1
CODING TERMS

In order to write code, we need a *computer*. So, let's briefly discuss what a computer is. As you know, it is a machine (equipment with a purpose; a tool).

Computers were created to do a simple thing: they take in data (information), change the data in some way, and send out data. That's all.

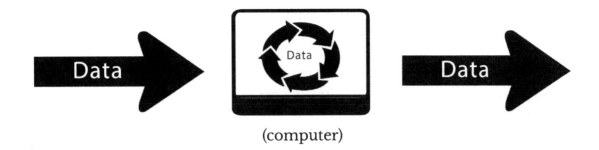

(computer)

As machines, some of the characteristics of computers include the following:

- They handle *data*. Again, data is information – such as words, symbols (something written that represents an amount, idea, or word), pictures, etc.

- They obey *instructions* (commands entered into them that perform certain tasks).

- They *automate* (perform actions without human interaction) tasks that would either take too long for a person to do or be too boring or repetitive.

- They *process* data. Process means to handle something through use of an established (and usually routine) set of procedures. When a computer displays the word "processing", it is simply saying, "Hold on while I perform some pre-established procedures." Processing refers to "taking actions with data." Searching through words to locate typos would be an example of processing data.

When computers perform actions, it is referred to as *executing* or *running*. For example, you can run a search on the internet by clicking the search button or you could execute an instruction by pressing enter on your keyboard.

THE PURPOSE OF COMPUTERS IS TO TAKE IN DATA, PROCESS IT AND SEND IT OUT.

The point where computers really started to become valuable to people was when it was worked out how to install programs on them.

Install means to put something inside a computer that the computer can then use.

Programs are sets of written instructions, entered into a computer by people, that make it execute specific tasks. Installing a program means to put it into a computer so that the program can execute. For example, you could install a program by transferring the data that makes up the program from the internet to your computer.

Behind every action you perform on a computer, there is a program. Common programs you have probably used before include:

- Microsoft Word (a program that allows you to type documents)

- Google Chrome (a program that helps you search the internet)

- iTunes (a program used to organize and listen to music)

Programs are written in a *programming language*. A programming language is an organized system of words, phrases, and symbols that lets you create programs. Just as there are many languages used by people across the world, there are different types of programming languages. In fact, there are over a thousand programming languages (though only about ten account for the majority of languages used).

In the same way that hammers and ladders have specialized utilizations, each programming language has different uses. For example, some programming languages were designed mainly to improve websites, while others were made for creating computer games.

The instructions inside these programs are referred to as *code*. Most code originally looks similar to English and is then translated down to instructions composed of the 1s and 0s that computers understand (called *machine language*).

For example, to have a computer display the words "Hello!" on your screen using Python (the popular computer programming language covered in this book that can be used to create programs and websites), the code is written as:

```
print("Hello!")
```

When someone says "program a computer" or "do some coding," they are just saying, "Write a set of instructions into a computer, using a programming language, that will result in specific actions being performed when that set of instructions is called for."

A *computer programmer* is one who engages in computer programming (writing code that results in programs). Programmers are also referred to as *coders*, *software developers*, and *software engineers*.

Coders create *software*, which is just another word for "program" or "application". These terms are all interchangeable – though "app" (abbreviation of application) is usually used to refer to programs (applications; software) on a mobile device (like a cell phone).

Computer programs are saved as *files*. As you may already know, files are collections of data stored on a computer. Files each have their own name and contain their own data, and they often are collected together in a *folder*. Folders are used to organize files on a computer and are given their own name. Another word for folder is *directory*. For example, an application could consist of multiple files all saved in the same directory (folder).

WHAT IS PYTHON?

Python is one of the most-used programming languages in the world. It was designed to look similar to English so that it is easier to read and write than some other overly technical languages.

Python is often used to create websites, analyze data, and automate tasks, but it can also be used for many other tasks, like building apps or controlling robots.

One of Python's key strengths is that it is versatile and flexible, meaning it can be used in a wide range of fields, from science to web development. It also has a large community of users who share tools, making it easier for new learners to find help and resources.

Here are some real-world uses of Python:

- Spotify: Python helps the service recommend songs and podcasts based on listening habits, while also keeping streams smooth for millions of users.

- NASA: uses Python to process and visualize data from space missions, aiding scientific research and analysis.

- Netflix: Python helps suggest shows and movies while managing video streams to ensure fast and reliable playback.

- Uber: utilizes Python to calculate ride prices, optimize driver routes, and analyze traffic patterns in real-time.

- Industrial Light & Magic (ILM): uses Python to automate animation processes, helping create special effects for blockbuster movies.

ORIGINS OF PYTHON

In 1989, the Dutch computer programmer Guido van Rossum began developing Python. He released the first version of it (version number 0.9.0) in 1991. (It was named 0.9 instead of 1 to indicate that it was still in an early, experimental stage and not yet a "full" release – Python 1.0 was released in 1994.) After its initial release, Python expanded to include other developers and contributors starting in the mid-1990s, with significant community involvement by the time Python 2.0 was released in 2000.

While at Google from 2005 to 2012, Guido van Rossum spent half his time working on Python, focusing on refining and enhancing the language. His efforts during this period helped Python grow in popularity, contributing to improvements in performance and usability.

(Guido van Rossum)

In the Python community, van Rossum was known as the "Benevolent Dictator For Life" (BDFL). BDFL referred to the fact that he continued to oversee the Python development process, making ultimate decisions where necessary. He was intimately involved in Python's development throughout much of its history, from its creation in 1989 until he stepped down as the BDFL in 2018. After stepping down, he took a less active role in Python's management, though he remains a respected figure in the community, and the language would not exist without him.

Mr. von Rossum was a big fan of the famous British comedy group, "Monty Python" (creators of the TV show "Monty Python's Flying Circus" and several popular films), and so the language was named in homage to them.

<u>WHERE DO YOU WRITE YOUR CODE?</u>

As you know, all software (applications; programs) are made up of code. As a user (the person using software), you do not see the code. So where is it and how is it written? Well, the three most common types of programs that developers use to write their code in are:

1) **Integrated Development Environment (IDE):** A *development environment* is a set of tools and software that is used for coding, testing, and debugging applications effectively. *Integrated* refers to the fact that the tools are combined into a single location, where they work together seamlessly. And so, an *IDE* is a software application that combines tools to streamline and simplify the process of writing, testing, and managing code in one unified location. For example, Visual Studio (available from Microsoft) is a popular IDE:

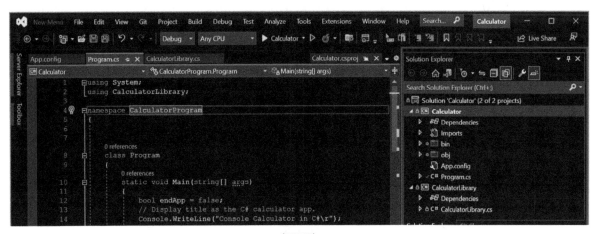

(IDE)

2) **Text editor:** A program used to write and edit text. Text editors are very basic – meaning, the text is typically plain with no effects. This is technically different

from a word processor, which is a program on a computer that allows you to create, format (design the style and layout), modify, and print documents. While text editors can be used to write code, word processors cannot. Instead, word processors have more functionality (the ability to perform a wider array of actions) than text editors. Below on the left you can see Microsoft Word (a word processor), while Notepad (on the right) is a text editor.

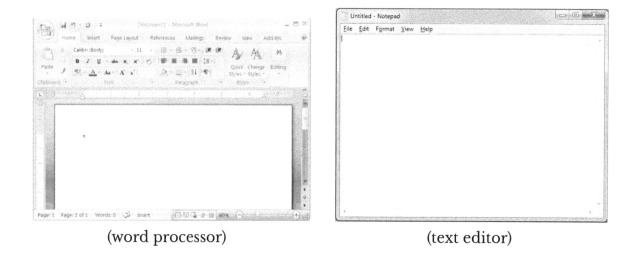

(word processor)   (text editor)

3) **Code editor:** A program that can be used to write/edit code. Code editors are in between IDEs and text editors in terms of features (functions built into an application) – they have fewer features than an IDE but more than a text editor. One of the most popular code editors is Notepad++ (plus plus). As an example, the popular IDE Visual Studio has a feature called "LiveShare", which allows developers to share their code with others as it is being written. This feature is not included in the code editor Notepad++. On the other hand, Notepad++ has a useful feature called "auto-completion" which suggests various options for completing the code you are typing. For example, when you type *pr*, auto-completion may suggest *print*. This feature does not exist in the text editor Notepad.

(code editor)

<u>IDLE</u>

IDLE stands for "Integrated Development and Learning Environment".

IDLE was designed by Guido van Rossum to be a simple IDE for Python, aimed at beginners, with a focus on ease of use and learning. He named it IDLE in honor of Eric Idle, one of the founding members of Monty Python.

Whereas most IDEs can be used to write programs in several different computer languages, IDLE is only used to write programs in Python. It was intended to be a simple development environment suitable for beginners, especially in an educational setting. We will use IDLE throughout this book.

OPERATING SYSTEM

An *operating system* is a special-purpose (made for exact applications and reasons) computer program that supports the computer's basic functions, such as scheduling tasks, running other computer programs, and controlling peripherals (external devices, such as keyboards, mice, and displays).

Computer programs typically require that an operating system already be installed before they can function on that computer.

Nearly all computers available today come with an operating system already installed when they are purchased because manufacturers install it ahead of time. Some operating systems are free and others require payment.

The two most-used operating systems are Windows (by Microsoft) and macOS (by Apple).

SHELL

In computing, the term *shell* refers to the outer layer between the user and the operating system, similar to its meaning in everyday English. It is a program that provides an interface (a point where two systems connect) for the user to issue commands to the operating system. Users can also write and execute code directly in a shell.

IDLE includes both a Python shell and a text editor, each serving a different purpose. The shell lets users type commands and immediately see the results, which is useful for quick testing or trying out code one step at a time. On the other hand, the text editor is where you can write longer programs and save them to run at a later time. Both are part of IDLE, making it a useful tool for both experimenting with code and building full programs.

In IDLE, the shell looks like this:

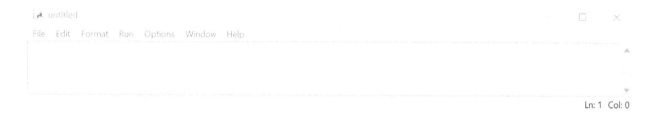

And the Python text editor looks like this:

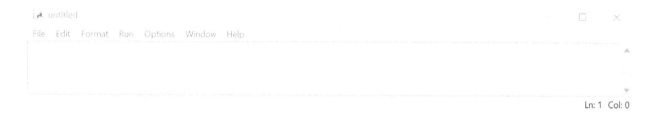

FILE PATHS

Characters are letters, numbers, and symbols – such as those found on a keyboard.

The route to a file is written with characters, and such a route is called a *file path*. The file path is the address of a file and specifies the exact location of a file. It provides a "path" to the file.

File paths say things like, "You can find the file named 'Winter' inside the folder named 'Poems', which is inside the C drive." (A *drive* is simply a location where data is stored, and the *C drive* is where most files and software are stored on a computer.)

The various components of a path are separated by a text character that is not part of the name of a directory (folder) or a file. Usually, this character is a slash (/), backslash (\ ) or colon (:).

The \ (backslash) symbol separates the different parts of a collection of electronic documents (files) in computers, and it was originally created as an aid to organizing and finding the various files you might store on a computer. In a file path, backslashes are used to show that one item is below another (in terms of hierarchy).

15

A *hierarchy* refers to arranging things according to rank or status. It refers to organizing items according to their relative importance or characteristics. *Storage hierarchy* refers to a system where various data storage devices are given a hierarchical importance ranking in terms of how they are used.

The primary factor influencing a given device's ranking is its response time (how long the device takes to return a requested piece of stored data when the computer requests the data). Faster response times are ranked "higher" and so are loaded/executed before others.

In a file path, the item on the left is "above" the one on the right. If we take our earlier example, the file path would be written as: **C:\Poems\Winter**

Written documents, pictures, and videos are examples of different types of *file formats*. The data in these various file formats is organized in a specific way, usually based on how the data will be used by various processes the computer does. For example, the data in a file that is a written document will be organized in a very different way than the data in a file that is a video.

A common file format is "PDF", which stands for "Portable Document Format". It is a file format developed by the software company Adobe in the 1990s to ensure consistent display of files regardless of what computer they are being displayed on.

File formats are indicated by their *extension*, which is code that states what the file format is (text, image, video, etc.). Extensions are tacked on at the end of the file's name. Let's say you have a file entitled "Contract" and it's stored as a PDF; the file would be named "Contract.pdf" (with .pdf being the extension). Another common file format and extension is ".txt" (short for "text file"). This is a file type that is pure, unformatted (no special design; plain) text. If you have ever used the application Notepad, it saves and runs .txt files.

The file extension for Python programs is *.py.*

VALUE TYPES

A *value* refers to the specific piece of data stored in a program (such as a number or text).

Value type (also referred to as *data type*) is a classification that specifies the kind of value a piece of data can hold (such as a number, text, or true/false statement) and how it can be used in programming.

Whereas a data type defines what kind of data you can use and the rules for how it behaves, a value is an actual example of that type. For example, 5 is a value which is part of the number data type.

Here are the main value types (data types) that are built into the Python programming language:

- **Number**: A type of value used to represent any kind of number, including whole numbers (called *integers*) or decimal numbers (called *floats*). EXAMPLE: A person's age, such as 39 (an integer), or a temperature, such as 98.6 (a float), are both number value types.

- **String**: A sequence of characters (like letters, numbers, or symbols) enclosed in quotation marks. EXAMPLE: "I love spicy Thai food!" is a string, representing a sentence of text.

- **Boolean**: A value that can only be either True or False (often used to make decisions within programs). EXAMPLE: In a program asking if it is raining, is_raining = True means that it is raining, while is_raining = False means it is not.

- **None**: A special value in Python used to show that something is empty or that no value has been assigned. It represents "nothing" or "no data". EXAMPLE: If a program asks for the user's name but they haven't provided it yet, the program could store that missing information as None, meaning there is "no name given".

- **List**: A collection of items arranged in a specific order. Lists can hold any type of data and are able to be changed after they are created. EXAMPLE: A shopping list, ["eggs", "milk", "bread"], is a list containing strings (text items).

- **Tuple**: Similar to a list, but tuples cannot be changed once created. Tuples are also used to store ordered collections of items. EXAMPLE: A tuple representing coordinates, (40.7128, -74.0060), holds a pair of numbers for a location.

- **Set**: A collection of unique items (meaning, each item appears only once). Sets are unordered, which means there is no specific order to the items. EXAMPLE: A set of favorite fruits might look like {"apple", "banana", "orange"}, where no fruit is repeated.

- **Dictionary**: A *key-value pair* is a set of two related pieces of information where the *key* is a unique identifier (name; label) and the *value* is the data associated with that key.

EXAMPLE: {"name": ["Alice", "Bob"], "age": [30, 25], "occupation": ["Engineer", "Doctor"]} is a dictionary where Alice and Bob are the keys, and 30, 25, Engineer and Doctor are the values.

- **Range:** A sequence of numbers. A range creates a list of numbers from a starting point to an ending point. EXAMPLE: range(1, 10) creates a sequence of numbers from 1 to 9.

- **Float:** A specific kind of number that represents decimal values (numbers with a fractional part). EXAMPLE: A person's height written as 5.9 is a float value type since it includes a decimal.

These data types will make more sense as we write them out in actual code later in this book, and we will take a deeper dive into these technical terms, but for now you have the basic definitions in place.

CHALLENGES

At the end of most chapters, we have included an "END OF CHAPTER CHALLENGE." These are opportunities for you to put together all that you studied in each chapter. At times you will also be instructed to figure out solutions to problems on your own.

Working software developers are often assigned projects and tasks they have never done before and so a key element of the job is researching solutions online.

Some of these challenges will have you repeat tasks you have already performed. The reasons for such repetition are to provide you with an opportunity to create your own approach, and allow you to better understand and remember code through additional practice.

CODING TIPS

We are nearing the end of this chapter and you will be writing code in no time! If you run into any trouble while going through this book, here are some tips:

1. Make sure your code is written *exactly* as it is in the book. The smallest error in your code (such as a missing comma or an extra symbol) can wreck the whole program. Code must be exact for programs to run properly, so always meticulously check your code for errors.

2. Research online for solutions.

3. Ensure you understand all the terms being used – define any words you do not understand. Misunderstood terms can prevent understanding and cause mistakes, so research for definitions when needed.

4. You can contact The Tech Academy through our website and ask for assistance here: learncodinganywhere.com

Now that we have prepared you for what to expect, and laid the basic foundation of coding terms and concepts, we can begin writing code!

CHAPTER 2
GETTING STARTED WITH PYTHON

It is time to get our hands dirty and write some code! From now on, each chapter will have you perform actions on your computer – you will actually *do* things. We have written all assignments (things you are expected to do on your computer) **in bold in a different font.**

And so, here is your first assignment:

1. **Download and install Python here:** python.org/downloads

   (Ensure to select the most recent version of Python.)

2. **Go to the "Downloads" folder on your computer and open the Python file to install it.**

3. **If there are checkboxes for "Use admin privileges when installing py.exe" and "Add python.exe to PATH", check both of these like this:**

   ☑ Use admin privileges when installing py.exe

   ☑ Add python.exe to PATH

4. **Complete all of the installation steps, starting with clicking "Install Now".**

Now that we have Python installed, let's open up IDLE! One of the easiest ways to do so is by searching "IDLE" on your computer by opening the search bar at the bottom of your screen and typing "IDLE".

Complete these actions:

1. **Open up IDLE.**

2. **Write this code:**

```
>>> print ('Hello, World!')
```

3. **Press Enter.**

Well done! Notice that "Hello, World!" is now printed. This is called *returning a value*. The value that has been returned, in this case, is the string "Hello, World!"

The three angle brackets (>>>) indicate where to type commands in IDLE.

Now, complete these actions:

1. Write this code in IDLE:

```
>>> print (Hello, World!)
```

(Without using quotation marks.)

2. Press Enter.

Oops! There was an error. That was intentional to show the importance of *syntax*. Every spoken language has a general set of rules for how words and sentences should be structured. These rules are known as the syntax of that particular language. In programming languages, syntax serves the same purpose. Syntax is the rules you must follow when writing code. As you know, there are many languages you can use to program a computer and each language has its own syntax. Failing to use the syntax of a particular language correctly can mean that whatever you are designing will not work at all.

VARIABLES

As a reminder, *value* refers to the specific piece of data stored in a program (such as a number or text).

A *variable* is a symbol or name that represents a value. In math, variables like "X" or "Y" are used to represent numbers in equations. Such as, "X + 2 = 5." (In this case, X is 3.)

In programming, variables store data values (such as numbers, text, or other types of information). They are called "variables" because their values can change (vary) as the program runs.

When coding, to *declare* a variable means to create it by giving it a name, so that it can store values later in the program.

Here is an example using pseudocode (words and symbols that look similar to code but are just normal English – not actual code):

```
START
DECLARE variable 'age'
SET 'age' to 25
DISPLAY 'age'
SET 'age' to 30  (this changes the value from 25 to 30)
DISPLAY 'age'
END
```

This "program" declares a variable called age, sets its value to 25, displays 25, changes the value to 30, and then displays 30. Now consider this image, which shows variable names and values:

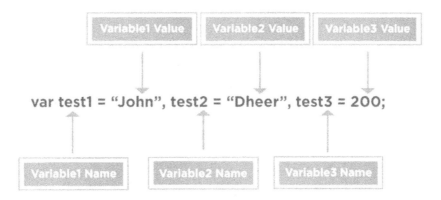

A common action in coding is to assign (declare) variables and they are key in every programming language. Let's assign a variable in Python by completing these actions:

1. Write this code in IDLE:

```
>>> J = 50
```

2. Press Enter.

Excellent work! You have just declared a variable by assigning the value 50 to the variable J.

As a note, there are certain words you cannot use as variables. These are called *reserved words* or *keywords*.

Examples of keywords are: "True" and "False" – which are used in Python to show the result of a comparison. For example, a comparison that checks "is 4 bigger than 2?" would result in True.

The reason you cannot use reserved words (keywords) is that they already mean something else – they are *reserved* for Python. If you're interested, here is a link to a list of the reserved words (keywords) in Python:

w3schools.com/python/python_ref_keywords.asp

Let's return the value stored in the variable J by completing these actions:

1. Write this code in IDLE:

```
>>> print (J)
```

2. Press Enter.

Good job! The value 50 is returned.

Now, let's try returning the value 50 with a lowercase j instead of an uppercase J to see what happens:

1. Write this code in IDLE:

```
>>> print (j)
```

2. Press Enter.

We get an error! This is because Python is *case-sensitive*. Case-sensitive means that it matters whether your code is capitalized or lowercase.

Your code must match what you wrote originally, or must match the Python documentation (the official instructions from the creators of Python that include all rules, syntax, procedures, etc.). Your original variable was a capital J, not a lowercase. Failing to utilize consistent capitalization and lowercasing can prevent the proper execution of code.

As a further example of case sensitivity of Python, do the following:

1. Write this code in IDLE:

```
>>> Print ('Well, hello there.')
```

(Write "Print" with a capital "P".)

2. Press Enter.

We get another error. This is because the print command is supposed to be written in lower-case.

MATH

The first computer programming languages ever created were primarily used to perform mathematical calculations because early computers were designed specifically to solve complex numerical problems. All modern programming languages can be used for this same purpose.

In mathematics, an *operator* is a symbol used to carry out a computation (the act of figuring out the amount of something using math). There are several different kinds of operators, such as arithmetic operators like:

+ (add),

- (subtract),

/ (divide), and

* (multiply)

These arithmetic operators are used to perform math operations.

In programming, an operator is a symbol or keyword (special word used within a programming language that holds a particular meaning and function) that instructs the computer to perform a specific action on values, such as calculating, comparing, or manipulating (controlling; handling) data.

For example, in Python the *assignment operator* is "=" and is used to assign value to a variable. For instance, if we write X = 10, we are assigning the variable "X" the value "10".

24

Now let's perform some basic math with Python by completing these actions:

1. Write this code in IDLE:

```
>>> 1 + 1
```

2. Press Enter.

Well done! The value returned is 2.

Write this code in IDLE (pressing enter after each line):

```
>>> K = 5
>>> print (J + K)
```

Good job! The value returned is 55. That is because J (50) + K (5) = 55. (Please note: all of this code is being written assuming you are using the same file in which you assigned the variable J the value of 50 earlier.)

We can subtract numbers in Python too!

Write this code in IDLE and then press enter:

```
>>> 2 - 1
```

Wonderful job! The value returned is 1.

Write this code in IDLE and then press enter:

```
>>> print (J - K)
```

Great work! The value returned is 45.

We can of course multiply numbers in Python as well.

Write this code in IDLE and then press enter:

```
>>> 4 * 5
```

Excellent work! The value returned is 20.

Now, let's perform multiplication with variables.

Write this code in IDLE and then press enter:

```
>>> print (J * K)
```

Very well done! The value returned is 250.

And we can divide numbers with Python.

Write this code in IDLE and then press enter:

```
>>> 100 / 5
```

Good job! The value returned is 20.

Write this code in IDLE and then press enter:

```
>>> print (J / K)
```

Perfect! The value returned is 10.

As you have seen, we can perform math with variables. Let's take this a little further by completing these actions:

1. Write this code in IDLE, pressing enter after each line:

```
>>> weight = 150
>>> print("The user weighs", weight, "pounds.")
```

2. Next write this code, pressing enter after each line:

```
>>> weight = weight + 10
>>> print("The user gained 10 pounds and now weighs", weight, "pounds.")
```

3. Then write this code, pressing enter after each line:

```
>>> weight = weight - 15
>>> print("The user went on a diet, lost 15 pounds, and now weighs", weight, "pounds.")
```

Good job! This program starts with an initial weight, simulates a weight gain, and then a weight loss, while printing the results at each step.

END OF CHAPTER CHALLENGE

We have now reached the first challenge in this book. In this one, you are going to create some basic programs using the data covered in this chapter.

Perform these actions:

1. Create two variables, assign them the values of 15 and 35, add them together, and then print their sum.

2. Create a variable with your age, subtract 5 from it, and print the result.

CHAPTER 3
PYTHON PROGRAMS

In preparation for upcoming assignments, let's complete a quick refresher about some math terms. *Factors* are numbers that can multiply together to get another number. For example, 4 and 5 are factors of 20 because 4 × 5 = 20.

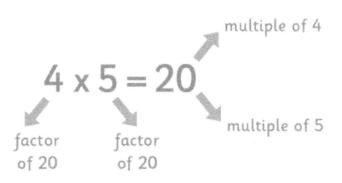

Superscripts are smaller characters, typically displayed toward the upper right of another number like this: **41²**

Superscripts usually indicate "power." Power refers to how many times a number is multiplied by itself. For example, **10⁴** means 10 to the fourth power – which is 10,000 (10 multiplied by 10 multiplied by 10 multiplied by 10).

A *notation* is a symbol or symbols used to represent numbers or amounts – such as an *E* placed at the end of a number. This notation means "10 to a given exponent." An *exponent* is the power to which a number is multiplied. In the 10^4 example given above, 4 is the exponent.

Here is a picture showing exponent and power (the total is 125):

A *floating point* is a specific way of representing large numbers. Instead of writing out the entire number, you can write the first part of it and then a factor to multiply it by.

This makes it so that by performing the multiplication, you get essentially the same number you would have by writing it out in full. When you do this, you move the decimal point in the number; hence the name "floating point."

For example, take the number three thousand, four hundred twenty-five. Written normally, it would be: 3425. Written in floating point notation, it could be: 3.425×10^3. Since 10^3 is 1000, this means "3.425 times 1000" or 3425.

A *float* is a type of data used by computers that is used to store numbers with a very high degree of accuracy. It is primarily used for mathematical purposes.

Let's say we want a shorter way to write 10,000. We could write 10E 4.

10E 4 means 10 X 10^4 (10 multiplied by 10 four times). (As a reminder, *E* stands for exponent, which is how many times a number is multiplied by itself.)

In Python, numbers are classified into two types: 1) integers (whole numbers), and 2) floating-point numbers (numbers with decimals).

The largest floating-point number Python can handle is 1.7976931348623157E+308. Any floating-point number larger than this is considered infinity (represented by *inf* in Python).

To give you an idea, 1.7976931348623157e+308 is a number so huge that it's far beyond the range of most calculators. It's about 179.77 quindecillion (a 1 followed by 308 zeros).

In Python, there are three special floating-point values that behave differently from regular numbers because they represent undefined or extreme conditions:

1) NaN (short for "Not a Number"): This value shows up when you try to do something that does not result in a real number (like dividing 0 by 0).

2) inf (positive infinity): This represents a number that is larger than Python's floating-point limit.

3) -inf (negative infinity): This represents a very large negative number, beyond Python's negative floating-point limit.

PYTHON DATA TYPES

As a reminder, some of the most common data types in Python are:

- String: A sequence of characters surrounded by quotation marks (e.g., `"Hello"`).

- Float: A number with a decimal point (e.g., `3.14`).

- Boolean: A value that can be either `True` or `False`.

- Integer: A whole number without a decimal point (e.g., `42`).

- List: An ordered collection of items, which can be of different data types (e.g., `[1, "apple", True]`).

So, let's put some of these into further use.

Write this code in IDLE and press enter after each line:

```
>>> A = "Odysseus returned home."
>>> A
```

Fantastic! "A" (the variable) returns the string. If you've noticed, we have used both single quotes and double quotes when writing strings in this book. For the most part, a quotation mark (") and an apostrophe (') are interchangeable in Python.

Write this code in IDLE and press enter after each line:

```
>>> B='Betty is excited!'
>>> B
```

Way to go! Notice that this time we did not include spaces in between the `=` and the rest of the text. That's because there is such a concept as *whitespace sensitivity*. White space literally refers to spaces. For example, there are five spaces (whitespace) between the words Apple and Orange here: Apple   Orange

Whitespace sensitivity refers to a programming language feature where the number of spaces in your code matters. In most instances, Python is not whitespace sensitive. Let's see this in action.

```
>>> C      =        'The cat is hungry.'
>>> C
```

It worked!

Even though Python is not white-space sensitive, it *is* indentation-sensitive. As you likely know, an indentation is the space or gap left at the beginning of a line of text to separate paragraphs or sections for clarity and organization. These are created by pressing the Tab key:

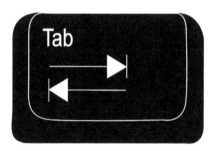

In order to describe the Tab key, you must first understand what a "spreadsheet" and a "table" are. A spreadsheet is a visual grid structure that allows you to organize, modify and analyze data. The data is stored in individual containers called cells. These cells are organized into rows and columns (each rectangle in this picture is a cell):

			Rows	
Columns				

31

Here is an example of a spreadsheet:

	A	B	C	D	
1	Country	Sales			
2	United States	7583			
3	United Kingdom	4359			
4	France	45995			
5	Germany	3933			
6	Spain	8738			
7	Italy	5239			
8	Greece	38282			
9					
10					

Sheet1 / Sheet2 / Sheet3

A set of rows and columns is called a table. In a more general sense, a table is information stored in a grid (lines that cross each other to form a series of squares and/or rectangles).

The "tab" in Tab key is short for "tabular" or "tabulator". "Tabular" means "of or related to a table", and it refers to data presented in columns or a table. A "tabulator" is a person or thing that arranges data in columns or tables, and then works with that data.

The Tab key moves the cursor (flashing bar on screen that indicates where to type) forward on the screen a set number of spaces – usually this is set to eight spaces. When you write a document and press the tab key, you indent your text (meaning, you move the text over around 8 spaces).

Python requires specific indentations at the beginning of some lines of code, which you will learn more about later in this book. This is mentioned here to explain why whitespace (spaces) at the beginning of your code causes errors. Let's see this in action.

Write this code in IDLE (before the letter "D", press Tab or type in extra spaces) and press enter :

```
>>>     D = 'The dog is thirsty.'
```

You will get this error "SyntaxError: unexpected indent". Again, this is because Python is indentation-sensitive.

FLOATS

As a reminder, a *float* is a number that has a decimal point. It is called "float" because the decimal point can "float", or move, to represent very large or very small numbers. For example, the number 0.0000123 can also be written as 1.23E-5, where the decimal point "floats" to show the same value.

To create a float variable, write this code in IDLE, pressing enter after each line:

```
>>> E = 10.75
>>> E
```

Very good!

BOOLEAN

As you know, *logic* refers to actions, behavior, and thinking that makes sense. When speaking about computers, logic is the rules that form the foundation for a computer in performing certain tasks. Computer logic is the guidelines the computer uses when making decisions.

Logical operators like "and", "or", and "not" are used to evaluate whether an expression is true or false.

George Boole was an English mathematician who developed *Boolean logic*. Boolean logic is a form of logic in which the only possible results of a decision are "true" and "false." There are not any vague or "almost" answers to a calculation or decision – black or white, no gray.

An example of Boolean logic would be answering questions with only "yes" or "no."

(George Boole)

Boolean logic is especially important for the construction and operation of digital computers because it is relatively easy to create a machine where the result of an operation is either "true" or "false." This is done by comparing two or more items – items that can only be "true" or "false."

Some common examples of such Boolean comparisons are "AND" and "OR". With the Boolean comparison called "AND", the comparison is true only if *all* of the involved comparisons are true.

Let's look at some examples to show how this works.

In the following AND comparison, the result is true: **5 is more than 3 AND 10 is more than 5.**

Let's break this down. There are three comparisons happening here:

1) Comparing 5 and 3 to see if 5 is larger than 3 (is 5 larger than 3?)

2) Comparing 10 and 5 to see if 10 is larger than 5 (is 10 larger than 5?)

3) Comparing the results of those two comparisons, using the Boolean comparison "AND" (are both comparisons true?). This is the overall comparison.

It is true that 5 is greater than 3, so the first comparison is true. It is also true that 10 is greater than 5 – so the second comparison is true as well.

A Boolean AND comparison is true if the other comparisons are all true – so in this example, the overall comparison is true, since the first comparison is true and the second comparison is also true.

In this next example, the result is false (not true): **5 is more than 7 AND 10 is more than 5**.

Even though 10 is more than 5, 5 is not more than 7 – so the overall comparison is not true.

A *condition* is an item that must be true before something else occurs. In the AND comparison above, these are the two conditions checked for:

1) 5 is more than 7

2) 10 is more than 5

They are conditions because the outcome is conditional upon (dependent on) these two comparisons.

A Boolean OR comparison checks for whether one or both conditions are true. Here is an example: **4 is less than 9 OR 8 is less than 7**.

The result would be true because at least one of the comparisons is true (4 is a smaller number than 9).

In the following example, the result would be false since neither is true: **8 is less than 4 OR 9 is less than 3**.

And in this example, the result would be true because one or both (in this case, both) are true: **7 is less than 8 OR 2 is less than 5**.

As a reminder, in writing instructions for a computer, we would use the greater and lesser symbols (> and <, respectively). For example: 7 > 3 means "seven is greater than three," and 4 < 9 means "four is less than nine."

So, for example, instead of 10 is greater than 2, we would write: **10 > 2**

And, again, if we wanted to say "greater than or equal to," we could use this symbol: >=

For example: **10 >= 8**

This would be true.

Here is a diagram showing Boolean logic applied to search terms:

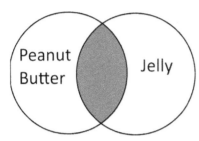

AND

Using AND, this search would only retrieve results with peanut butter and jelly.

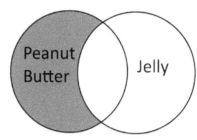

OR

Using OR, this search would retrieve results with peanut butter, with jelly, and with both.

NOT

Using NOT, this search would retrieve results with peanut butter, and exclude those with jelly or PB with jelly.

Like virtually all other programming languages, the Boolean values in Python are true and false.

To utilize Boolean logic, write this code in IDLE, pressing enter after each line:

```
>>> E = 10
>>> E is 10
```

Great work! As you can see, *True* is returned.

Now write this code in IDLE and press enter:

```
>>> E is 25
```

Precisely! *False* is returned.

Next, write this code in IDLE and press enter:

```
>>> E is not 50
```

Good work! As you can see, *True* is returned.

Now, let's utilize the greater than symbol (>).

Write this code in IDLE and press enter:

```
>>> 25 > 10
```

Excellent work! Here we stated that 25 is more than 10, which is, of course, True.

Write this code in IDLE and press enter:

```
>>> 10 > 25
```

Great job! We flipped it around here and said that 10 was more than 25 – this is False.

As a reminder, the symbol "<" means "less than."

Write this code in IDLE and press enter:

```
>>> 25 < 10
```

Very good! In this code, we stated that 25 is less than 10, which, as you know, is False.

Write this code in IDLE and press enter:

```
>>> 10 < 25
```

Wonderful job! We wrote that 10 is less than 25, which is True.

DOUBLE EQUAL SIGNS

In Python, we can utilize double equal signs (==) to compare values. Specifically, the "==" symbol checks whether the value on the left side of the symbol is equal to the value on the right side. The result of this comparison is always True or False.

When the == symbol is used to check for equality, it is usually structured like this: [first item to be compared] == [second item to be compared]

For example: (10 + 5) == 15

In this example, we are asking the computer to check whether the result of adding 5 and 10 is equal to 15. The result would be True.

Another example: (10 + 20) == 15

Here, the program would return False since (10 + 20) is not equal to 15.

Like all code, this is best understood by writing it out ourselves.

Write this code in IDLE and press enter:

```
>>> 500 == 500
```

Very good job! Here we wrote that 500 is equal to 500, which is True.

Write this code in IDLE and press enter:

```
>>> 500 == 250
```

Great work! We stated that 500 is equal to 250, which is, of course, False.

NOT EQUAL TO (!=)

In many programming languages, the symbol ! means "not." In Python, the operator != means "check that the value on the left is *not* equal to the value on the right." Let's put this into use.

Write this code in IDLE and press enter:

```
>>> 100 != 50
```

Perfect! The statement that 100 is not equal to 50 is True.

Write this code in IDLE and press enter:

```
>>> 100 != 100
```

Good job! The statement that 100 is not equal to 100 is False.

GREATER THAN OR EQUAL TO (>=)

The operator ">=" means "check that the value on the left is equal to or greater than the value on the right." Let's try this out.

Write this code in IDLE and press enter:

```
>>> 10 >= 10
```

Excellent work! The statement "10 is greater than or equal to 10" is True because they are equal.

Write this code in IDLE and press enter:

```
>>> 20 >= 10
```

Very good! The statement "20 is greater than or equal to 10" is True because 20 is a greater value.

Write this code in IDLE and press enter:

```
>>> 5 >= 10
```

Wonderful job! The statement "5 is greater than or equal to 10" is False.

The opposite of the >= operator is <=, which is "less than or equal to" and means "check that the value on the left is less than or equal to the value on the right."

You can see this in action by writing this code in IDLE, pressing enter after each line:

```
>>> A = 1000
>>> A <= 500
    False
>>> A <= 1000
    True
>>> A <= 5000
    True
```

Phenomenal work! The code in this section of the book illustrates Boolean logic.

COMMENTING CODE

Commenting code is the act of leaving notes in your code that explain various points for yourself and/or others. The comments are not run in the program but are read by people when viewing the code directly, so they can understand the code better.

Writing comments for each block (section) of code is considered best practice – it not only clarifies the code for others, it assists you in remembering the original purpose and meaning of the code.

To write comments in Python, you simply add "#" at the beginning of the statement. The comment should be written above the code.

In IDLE, write this code and press enter after each line:

```
>>> #Checks if 365 is greater than 182
>>> 365 > 182
```

Way to go! The code ran, and your comment was not printed – it remained as a "behind the scenes" explanation.

SCRIPTS

Scripts are small programs that automate tasks or make websites interactive by responding to user actions.

For example, a script could be written that updates the shopping cart total on a website when a user adds or removes items without needing to reload the entire page. So, let's write one!

To do so, we are going to transition from the shell to the text editor. In IDLE, navigate to "File" (in the top left corner) and click "New File". This allows you to work in the text editor to create a program to run, rather than working directly in the shell. Put another way, in the shell, one line of code is written and executed at a time, whereas in the text editor, multiple lines of code can be written and then executed all at once (from top to bottom). Simply put, the text editor within IDLE allows for stronger and longer programs.

Complete these actions:

1. Write this code in the text editor:

```
a = 5
b = 10
result = a + b
print(result)
```

2. Save the file with the .py extension (Python code files written in the editor must always be saved prior to execution). There are multiple ways you can save your code:

   a. Click "File", select "Save As...", name the file, and then click "Save". Or,

   b. Press "Ctrl" and "S" at the same time, and save it that way. For Mac users, press "Command" (⌘) and "S" at the same time.

3. Run your program. There are a couple of ways to execute your code after saving it:

   a. Click "Run" and then select "Run Module". (In this sense, a *module* is a file containing Python code that can be run as a standalone program or imported into other programs.)

   b. Press the F5 key. On a Mac, press "Function" (fn) + F5.

   From now on in this book, when we direct you to execute your code in the text editor, save it and run it as detailed above.

Fabulous work! The program should run and return the value 15.

IF STATEMENTS

A *conditional statement* is a programming element that allows the execution of certain blocks of code based on whether a specific condition or set of conditions evaluates to true or false, enabling decision-making within a program.

An *if statement* is a type of conditional statement that specifies that a section of code is to be executed *if* a condition is true.

Write this code in the text editor (the second line should automatically indent, which is what we want), save the file, and run it:

```
X = 100
if X > 25:
    print('X is the winner!')
```

Very good job! The program will now print "X is the winner!" because the if statement (a conditional statement) evaluated to true due to the fact that X *is* greater than 25.

Write this code in the text editor, save the file, and run it:

```
if Y == 20:
    print('20 is equal to Y.')
```

We get an error message. This is because we need to define the variable Y.

In the text editor, write this code *above* the if statement you just wrote, save the file, and run it:

```
Y = 20
```

Good job! It now runs and prints "20 is equal to Y."

STRINGS

As a reminder, a *string* is a sequence of characters used to represent text data, usually defined within single or double quotes.

Write this code in the text editor (you can write your name instead - just include capital letters), save the file, and run it:

```
name = 'GiDeOn'
print(name.lower())
```

Very good! Your name is now displayed in lower case.

Now add this line of code at the bottom of your program, save the file, and run it:

```
print(name.upper())
```

Awesome work! Now we have displayed the name in all caps.

END OF CHAPTER CHALLENGE

Perform these actions:

1. Write a program within IDLE that utilizes each of these operators:
   a. >=   (greater than or equal to)
   b. <=   (less than or equal to)
   c. ==   (equal to)
   d. !=   (not equal to)

2. Store your name in a string variable, then print a welcome message in ALL CAPS, like: "GREETINGS, [YOUR NAME]!"

3. Write a program that stores the price of an item as a float (e.g., 19.99), then prints the price with a message like "The item costs $19.99."

4. Create a boolean variable is_raining set to True or False, and print a message based on whether it's raining.

5. Use an if statement to check if a temperature is above 30 degrees, and print "It's hot outside!" if the condition is met.

CHAPTER 4
PYTHON FUNCTIONS

A *function* is a reusable block of code in Python that performs specific actions or tasks. You execute a function by calling it.

To *call* a function means to execute it so that it performs its defined task. Calling a function is also known as *invoking* the function. In coding, invoking (or calling) means "causing a set of actions to be carried out."

In Python, we create functions using the *def* keyword.

As a reminder, *keywords* are reserved words (words that cannot be used as variables or for other names because they already perform a function and hold a meaning in Python) that identify actions to be performed in Python.

The def keyword is specifically used to define a new function.

The basic syntax for writing a Python function is: the def keyword, then the function name, followed by parentheses (), and a colon, as follows:

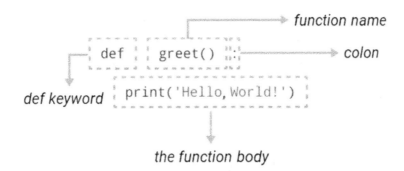

Functions are valuable because they allow for code reusability. Once defined, you can invoke a function multiple times, making your code more efficient and organized.

In coding, an *object* is something that has state (condition; attribute) and behavior (action; procedure). For example, a "dog" object could have "awake" as its state and "barking" as its behavior.

In Python, functions are also considered objects, which means they can be assigned to variables and have states and behaviors.

A *method* is something an object can do – it is a named sequence of events.

A method should always have a meaningful name, such as CalculateIncomeTax (not Method_1 or something else that's non-descriptive), that way you can get an idea of what the method is supposed to do from just reading the name. The `.lower()` and `.upper()` code we wrote earlier are both methods built into Python.

Now that we have all these terms under our belt, let's write a function.

Write this code in the text editor (using a name of your choice), save the file, and run it:

```
name = "Madeline"
def greet():
    print('Hello, ' + name + '. Welcome to my program!')

greet()
```

Very good job! We created a basic function here, and then called (executed; ran) it with greet().

ARRAYS

An *array* is a collection of data, arranged in rows and columns. It is a group of related things that are stored together in a sequence.

In coding, arrays are used to organize items in a logical way. They can be quite simple or quite complex.

A simple array would be something like the numbers 7, 3 and 15. It could be written out like this: **[7, 3, 15]**

These three pieces of data are called *elements* – they are the elements of the array. Another word for the data in an element is *value*. The first element in the array here has a value of "7".

A system is needed for identifying each element of an array. The simplest method for this is to start numbering them at zero starting at the left position and count up from there. In the above example, the element "7" would be at position 0, "3" would be at position 1 and "15" would be at position 2.

Another word for the position of an element is the *index* of the element – for the above example of an array, index 0 is "7", index 1 is "3", etc.

Each element, therefore, has two properties: its index and its value.

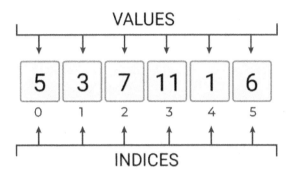

(The plural of *index* is *indices* or *indexes*.)

Let's say you have three pictures of your cat and you could save them in an array: "CatPic1", "CatPic2" and "CatPic3".

The array would look like this: **["CatPic1,""CatPic2,""CatPic3"]**

Here, the element at index 1 has a value of "CatPic2".

Arrays are objects (as a reminder, objects can have properties [characteristics] and methods [actions]).

MODULES

A *module* is a pre-made collection of Python code for your use. It is code written by others that can enhance your program and save you time. Python has many modules that exist to assist developers. These modules have functions you can use to add functionality to your program.

Some functions come built into the Python language – like `.upper()` and `.lower()` that we wrote before (which can make strings uppercase or lowercase respectively) but other functions require you to import a module before they can be used. Importing a module just means adding the code of that module to your Python program so that the program can use it.

In order to write an array in Python, we need to import the array module.

CREATING AN ARRAY

Let's write a basic program that creates an array of integers (whole numbers), prints it, accesses and prints the first item, then demonstrates adding and removing items from the array.

Write this code in the text editor, save the file, and run it:

```python
import array

numbers = array.array('i', [10, 20, 30, 40, 50])
print("Here is the full numbers array:", list(numbers))
print("Here is the first item in the array:", numbers[0])
numbers.append(60)
print("Here is the array after adding the number 60:", list(numbers))
numbers.remove(30)
print("Finally, here is the array after removing 30:", list(numbers))
```

Very good! As a note, in this program, the 'i' (which stands for 'integer') is used in the "array" module to tell Python to store only whole numbers in the array, helping to keep storage efficient and ensuring only integers are added. If we didn't include the 'i', an error would occur because the array module needs a specific data type to know what kind of values the array will store. In everyday English, *append* means to add something to the end of something else, and in programming, it refers specifically to adding an item to the end of a list or array, expanding its contents.

LISTS

In Python, *lists* are flexible collections that can store different data types (numbers, strings, Booleans, etc.) within the same list, while arrays can only store numerical data and require a single data type (such as integers *or* floats), making lists more versatile overall but less efficient for numerical data.

Here is the proper syntax for creating a Python list: `Name_of_list = [item1, item2]`, etc.

Write this code in the text editor (include whatever band names you choose), save the file, and run it:

```python
best_bands_list = ["The Beatles", "Rolling Stones", "Led Zeppelin", "Beach Boys"]

print("Here is a list of the best bands: ", best_bands_list)
```

Now let's display a string with a single band name from our list by specifying its index. (Note: our list here is technically an array.)

Add this line of code at the bottom of your program, save the file, and run it:

```
print(best_bands_list[0], "is my favorite band!")
```

Fabulous! The same can be done with the remaining items of the list by calling out each item in the array by its index number: [1] for Rolling Stones, [2] for Led Zeppelin, and [3] for Beach Boys.

CHANGING LISTS

To change a list, we specify which item we want to replace or change. First, let's add something to the list.

Add this line of code at the bottom of your program (again, you can write a band of your choice), save the file, and run it:

```
best_bands_list.append("The Doors")
print(best_bands_list[4], "was just added onto the list.")
```

Very good! We appended a new band onto our list. Reminder, even though it is index number 4, it is the 5th band on the list, because lists and arrays always start at 0.

Now let's replace an item on the list.

Add this line of code at the bottom of your program (again, you can write a band of your choice), save the file, and run it:

```
best_bands_list[2] = "The Supremes"
print("Here is the updated list of the best bands: ", best_bands_list)
```

Good job! We removed Led Zeppelin and added The Supremes in their place.

TUPLES

Another type of list is called a *tuple*. A tuple is an ordered (sequenced), unchangeable collection of items grouped together.

The term originates from mathematics, where it is used to describe a sequence of elements, and is derived from Latin suffixes like "-uple" (like in "quadruple"), representing groups of items in specific amounts.

The difference between a "list" and a "tuple" is that tuples cannot be altered, and tuples use parentheses instead of square brackets. Tuples are immutable data types. "Immutable" means "unable to be changed."

Let's create a tuple.

Write this code in the text editor, save the file, and run it:

```
person_info = ("Danny", 35, "President")
print("Person Information:", person_info)
print("Name:", person_info[0])
print("Age:", person_info[1])
print("Occupation:", person_info[2])
```

Very well done! Now let's try to change Danny's age.

Write this line of code at the end of your program, save the file, and run it:

```
person_info[1] = 21
```

We get an error! Again, this is because tuples are immutable (not able to be altered).

DATES

Let's set a date in Python and then use the split() method to split apart the day, month and year.

49

```
def split_date(date):
    return date.split('/')

print(split_date("03/13/2030"))
```

Good work! This code defines a function that takes a date in MM/DD/YYYY format, splits it by slashes, and returns a list of the month, day, and year as separate items.

Now let's edit our code in the text editor as follows, then save the file, and run it:

```
def split_date(date):
    split_date = date.split('/')
    print("Month:", split_date[0])
    print("Day:", split_date[1])
    print("Year:", split_date[2])

split_date("03/13/2030")
```

Well done! This program performs the same basic functions as the preceding one, but displays the date in a clearer format.

CONCATENATING STRINGS

Concatenate means to link or join things together in a sequence, such as combining multiple pieces of text or strings into one continuous string in programming.

Let's concatenate (connect) strings so that the dates we entered are displayed with the day, month, and year.

Write this code in the text editor, save the file, and run it:

```
def split_date(date):
    split_date = date.split('/')
    print("Month: " + split_date[0] + ", Day: " + split_date[1] + ", Year: " + split_date[2])

split_date("03/13/2030")
```

50

Very good job! Notice that we added a space after each colon. If we didn't, the date would display right up against the colon – e.g., Year:2030, instead of Year: 2030.

Write this code in the text editor, save the file, and run it:

```
longer_name = "Alexander"
shorter_name = longer_name[2] + longer_name[3] + longer_name[5]
print("Full name:", longer_name)
print("Nickname:", shorter_name)
```

Excellent work! Can you see what this code does? You printed characters from a string using specific indices, and concatenated them using the + operator.

DIVISION FUNCTIONS

In older versions of Python, dividing two integers with the / operator would return an integer result, discarding anything after the decimal point. Now, Python automatically preserves the decimal part, so dividing integers with / gives a float (decimal) result.

If you'd like to remove everything after the decimal point, you can use the // operator instead of the normal / operator. This is called *floor division*, and it returns only the whole number part of the result, discarding the decimal. It is referred to as "floor division" because it "floors" (rounds down) the result to the nearest whole number, removing anything after the decimal point.

This will all make more sense by putting it into action.

Write this code in the text editor, save the file, and run it:

```
def demonstrate_division(a, b):
    normal_division = a / b
    print("Using / : ", a, "/", b, "=", normal_division, "(result is a float)")
    floor_division = a // b
    print("Using // : ", a, "//", b, "=", floor_division, "(result is a whole number)")
demonstrate_division(7, 3)
```

Very good! This code defines a function that takes two numbers, performs both normal division (/) to get a float result and floor division (//) to get a whole number result, then prints each outcome with an explanatory message. Finally, it calls the function with 7 and 3 as example inputs to demonstrate the difference between the two division types.

END OF CHAPTER CHALLENGE

Perform these actions:

1. Define a function that takes two numbers, adds them and returns their sum.

2. Create an array of your five favorite colors and print each color.

3. Write a list, print it out, change an item on the list, and print it out again.

4. Define a tuple with three numbers and write code to concatenate them into a string that says "The numbers are: [number1, number2, number3]."

CHAPTER 5
METHODS AND FUNCTIONS

Let's learn some new methods and functions!

You can change the case of letters through using the `.swapcase()` method.

Write this code in the text editor, save the file, and run it:

```
name = "Scout"
name = name.swapcase()
print(name)
```

Excellent work!

INPUT

The `input()` function allows the user to enter (input) information.

Write this code in the text editor, save the file, and run it:

```
date = input('Enter a date here: ')
print('This is the date you entered: ' + date)
```

Awesome work! (Make sure to enter a date and press enter.)

STRIP() METHOD

We can get rid of spaces and tabs from strings by using the `.strip()` method.

Write this code in the text editor (placing extra spaces or tabs before and after your name), save the file, and run it:

```
name = input("Enter your first name with extra spaces and tabs here: ")
cleaned_name = name.strip()
print("Hello,", cleaned_name + "!")
```

Great work! The empty space before and after your name was eliminated.

ESCAPE CHARACTER

An *escape character* is a symbol in programming that signals the computer to interpret the following character differently, often for formatting or special functions. It is called "escape" because it lets characters "escape" their usual meaning to perform special functions.

In Python, this is a backslash: \

Here are some of the most common uses of escape characters in Python:

- New Line: \n – moves to the next line.
- Tab: \t – adds a tab space.
- Backslash: \\ – inserts a backslash.
- Single Quote: \' – allows single quotes within strings written with single quotes.
- Double Quote: \" – allows double quotes within double-quoted strings.

The escape character allows special formatting within strings (such as enabling new lines, tabs, and inclusion of otherwise restricted characters like quotes and backslashes). In order to understand the usefulness of escape characters, let's try writing a couple of lines of code without them.

Write this code in the text editor, save the file, and run it:

```python
print('Joe's house is bigger than Roger's but they're both nice.')
```

We get an error! We attempted to use apostrophes within a string enclosed in single quotes and it didn't work. Let's try another approach that does not work.

Write this code in the text editor, save the file, and run it:

```python
print("Leonardo da Vinci said, "Simplicity is the ultimate sophistication."")
```

Another error because we attempted to use double quotes inside a string written within double quotes.

We can fix this with escape characters.

Write this code in the text editor, save the file, and run it:

```
def demonstrate_escape_characters():
    print("This is a new line:\nSee, we're on the next line now!")
    print("Here is a tab:\tThis text is indented with a tab.")
    print("Here is a backslash: \\")
    print('Michelle\'s dog didn\'t bark at the cat.')
    print("\"Imagination is more important than knowledge.\" -Albert Einstein")
demonstrate_escape_characters()
```

Well done! As you can see, the backslash changed the execution of the character immediately following it.

ELSE STATEMENTS

As a reminder, an *if statement* is a conditional statement (code that executes only if a specific condition is met). If statements run specific code only if a certain condition is true, and we wrote one earlier on in this book.

The *else statement* defines a block of code that executes only if all preceding conditions are false, providing an alternative action. For example, if you pass the exam, celebrate; else, prepare for the next one.

Write this code in the text editor, save the file, and run it:

```
age = int(input("Enter your age: "))
if age >= 18:
    print("You are eligible to vote!")
else:
    print("You are not eligible to vote yet.")
```

Very good! You created a basic program that determines whether or not a user is old enough to vote.

Now, try this: Run the program again and type letters instead of numbers, such as "Twenty-five," and observe the result. You'll see an error! We'll address this in the next section.

ELIF

In Python, *elif* (short for "else if") is used to check additional conditions if the initial if statement is false, allowing for multiple condition checks in sequence.

The elif statement follows an if statement and, again, is executed only in the case that the if statement is found to be false. For example: 1) If: hungry, eat. 2) Elif: thirsty, drink. 3) Else: rest.

The `isdigit()` method in Python checks if all characters in a string are digits (0–9) and returns True if they are; otherwise, it returns False. This method is useful for validating that an input string represents a positive integer and doesn't contain letters, spaces, or special characters.

Let's expand the program we just wrote to account for incorrect user input.

Write this code in the text editor, save the file, and run it:

```python
def voting_eligibility():
    age_input = input("Enter your age: ")
    if age_input.isdigit():
        age = int(age_input)
        if age >= 18:
            print("You are eligible to vote.")
        else:
            print("You are not eligible to vote yet.")
    elif not age_input.isdigit():
        print("Please enter a valid number.")

voting_eligibility()
```

(In this program, `elif not` is used to check if the input is not a number – i.e., contains non-digit characters.)

Excellent work! But if the user enters something besides a digit, the program only states "Please enter a valid number." and then the program stops – meaning, the user is not given a chance to submit new input! We can fix that by adding a line at the bottom of our elif statement.

Add this line of code at the end of your elif statement:

```python
voting_eligibility()
```

Here is what your full code should now look like:

```python
def voting_eligibility():
    age_input = input("Enter your age: ")
    if age_input.isdigit():
        age = int(age_input)
        if age >= 18:
            print("You are eligible to vote.")
        else:
            print("You are not eligible to vote yet.")
    elif not age_input.isdigit():
        print("Please enter a valid number.")
        voting_eligibility()

voting_eligibility()
```

Notice that we are calling (executing; running) your function in two places: at the very end of the program *and* within the elif statement. Why? Two reasons: 1. We have to run the function, and we do that by calling it, but we have to write the function before calling it! That's why it is placed at the end (it is defined, *then* run). And, 2. We want the program to run again (start over) if the user enters incorrect data so that they can fix their error, and that's the reason we call the function within the elif statement as well.

TIME.SLEEP()

The `time.sleep()` function allows you to delay running a line of code by specified seconds or portions of seconds (as in a float – like 1.5). To use the `Time.Sleep()` function, you must first import the *time* module (which contains functions to work with time-related tasks).

Write this code in the text editor, save the file, and run it:

```python
import time
def delayed_message():
    delay = float(input("Enter the number of seconds you would like to delay: "))
    time.sleep(delay)
    print("That was a", delay, "second delay.")
delayed_message()
```

END OF CHAPTER CHALLENGE

Perform these actions:

1. Write a function that accepts user input.

58

2. Write a program that utilizes at least one escape character.

3. Write a conditional statement that includes: if, elif and else.

CHAPTER 6
LOOPS

In normal English, a *loop* is something that connects back to the beginning point.

In programming, a loop is a sequence of instructions that are continually repeated until an exact condition is achieved. Usually, it would be where a certain set of actions are performed by a computer program, then the program checks to see if it has reached the condition required for completion. If not, it starts over and repeats the set of actions. If so, it exits the loop and moves on to the next consecutive instruction in the computer program.

For example, you could direct the computer to search through a list of paint colors until the color "red" is found. The list the computer will search is this:
- Blue
- Yellow
- Red
- Orange
- White

Here is what it could look like in pseudocode:

Step 1: Get the next consecutive item in the list.

Step 2: Check whether the item equals "Red."

Step 3: If the item equals "Red," exit this loop.

Step 4: If the item is not equal to "Red," loop back to step 1.

When this loop is executed, it will run like this:

Step 1: Acquired "Blue."

Step 2: Checked if item "Blue" is equal to "Red"

Step 3: Item not equal to "Red." Did not exit the loop.

Step 4: Item not equal to "Red." Looped back to Step 1.

Step 1: Acquired "Yellow."

Step 2: Checked if item "Yellow" is equal to "Red."

Step 3: Item not equal to "Red." Did not exit the loop.

Step 4: Item not equal to "Red." Looped back to Step 1.

Step 1: Acquired "Red."

Step 2: Checked if item "Red" is equal to "Red."

Step 3: Item equal to "Red." Exited the loop.

In normal English, *iterate* means to do something repeatedly.

In coding, iterate has a similar meaning: to say or do something again; to repeat an action.

An *iteration* is the act of repeating. It means to go through a defined series of actions, repeating a certain number of times. Usually, this defined series of actions is repeated a certain number of times, or until a condition is met.

Computer programs are usually created in iterations: Coming up with a basic working version, reviewing the program for mistakes to correct and improvements to make, doing that work, and repeating. When the program works acceptably, this process ends.

In Python, the *while loop* means that "while (blank) is occurring, do (blank)."

A while loop is basically a repeating "if statement." Meaning, you are telling the computer to execute certain code repeatedly while a particular condition is present.

For example: While hungry, eat.

A while loop loops through a block of code for as long as a specified condition is true.

Here it a while loop diagrammed:

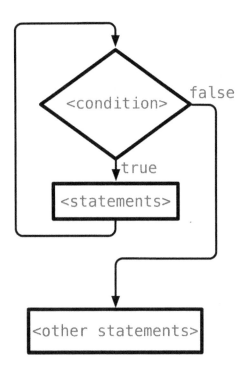

The -= operator is a subtraction assignment in Python. It means "subtract the right-hand value from the left-hand variable and then assign the result back to the variable." For example, in a video game, you could use player_health -= damage to reduce the player's health by the amount of damage taken.

Write this code in the text editor, save the file, and run it:

```
import time
countdown = 10
while countdown > 0:
    print(countdown)
    time.sleep(0.5)
    countdown -= 1
print("Blastoff!")
```

Exceptional job! This program initializes (starts; begins) a countdown from 10, prints each number with a 0.5-second delay between each number, and decrements (lowers; reduces) the countdown by 1 on each loop until it reaches 0, at which point it prints "Blastoff!" In this while loop, we are saying, "While countdown (10) is greater than 0, continue counting down." After the while loop is complete (once we hit a number 0), we display "Blastoff!"

break is a command used to immediately exit a loop, stopping any further iterations (repetitions) and moving on to the next part of the code outside the loop.

Now let's write a while loop that determines whether or not a user entered a positive number (a number greater than 0).

Write this code in the text editor, save the file, and run it:

```
def positive_number():
    while True:
        user_input = input("Enter a positive number: ")
        if user_input.isdigit() and int(user_input) > 0:
            print("Thank you! You entered this positive number:", user_input)
            break
        else:
            print("Invalid input. Please enter a positive number.")

positive_number()
```

Excellent work! Did you notice we used an if statement within the while loop? Conditional statements are commonly used within while loops to check conditions on each iteration, allowing the program to make decisions or handle different scenarios as the loop continues.

FOR LOOPS

A *for loop* is used to repeat a section of code a number of times.

For loops are used when the number of iterations is known.

For example: for each student in the class (25), provide a grade.

The for loop repeatedly executes instructions as long as a particular condition is true.

You can see a diagram of a for loop on the following page.

Here is a for loop:

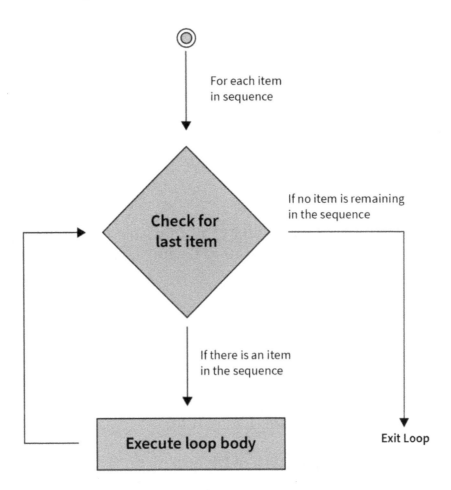

In Python, the `range()` function generates a sequence of numbers (typically used in loops) starting from a given number up to, but not including, a specified end number, with an optional step to skip numbers.

The variable "i" is commonly used in loops as a shorthand for *index* or *iterator*. As a reminder, an index is a position marker (number) that identifies the location of each element in a sequence, allowing specific elements to be accessed directly. An iterator is a tool in programming that goes through each element in a sequence (like a list or a range of numbers) one at a time in a defined order.

In loops, "i" is often used as a simple, standard variable to count each step or position in a sequence, helping to track where the program is in the loop and allowing access to elements based on their position. For example, in our earlier countdown timer, "i" could represent each number, allowing the program to print each step, like a countdown timer.

Actually, let's rewrite our earlier "while loop" countdown timer as a "for loop", so we can see this in action.

Write this code in the text editor, save the file, and run it:

```
import time
for i in range(10, 0, -1):
    print("Countdown:", i)
    time.sleep(0.5)
print("Liftoff!")
```

Awesome job! This for loop uses "i" as a variable to represent each step in a countdown sequence, decreasing from 10 to 1, with "i" displaying each number on screen before ending with "Liftoff!"

Again, *for loops* are used when you know the exact number of iterations needed or are iterating over a sequence (like a list or range), whereas a *while loop* is utilized when the loop should continue until a certain condition is met, which might vary in the number of iterations.

DICTIONARIES

A *dictionary* is a specialized type of list. In a dictionary, the first item is the *key* (a unique identifier for some item of data), and the second item is the *value* (the data that is identified by the key). Together, they are a *key-value pair*.

"Key-value pair" is abbreviated "KVP." A KVP is a set of two linked data items that (again) consists of: a key and the value. Again, the key is the unique name, and the value is its content. Collections of KVPs (i.e., dictionaries) are often used in computer programs.

Below is an example of a collection of KVPs that might be used in a computer program for a school. Here, the KEY is used to store the name of a course at the school, and the VALUE is the description of the course – this is a dictionary:

KEY	VALUE
INTRO_TO_PHYSICS	Basic physics principles.
WORLD_HISTORY	Global historical events.

ALGEBRA_I	Equations and graphing.
ENGLISH_LITERATURE	Study of literary works.
BIOLOGY	Cells and ecosystems.

Note that in this dictionary, you could not have a second Key-Value Pair that used the "BIOLOGY" key or "WORLD_HISTORY" key, because each key in a given collection of KVPs must be unique.

And so, a "dictionary" is "a key-value pair collection."

In a dictionary, multiple values can be assigned to one key. This can be useful because you can look up various values by their key. In the below example, each key has three values assigned to it:

KEY	VALUES
0	Eddard Stark | 35 years old | Male
1	Cersei Lannister | 32 years old | Female
2	Jon Snow | 18 years old | Male
3	Daenerys Targaryen | 20 years old | Female

Let's write a dictionary!

Write this code in the text editor, save the file, and run it:

```
birthdays = {
    "Jack": {"month": "August", "year": 1985},
    "Emily": {"month": "March", "year": 1983},
    "Violet": {"month": "July", "year": 2008},
    "Magnus": {"month": "March", "year": 2018},
    "Maxine": {"month": "July", "year": 1987}
}
print(birthdays)
```

Very well done! In this dictionary, the names are the keys and the month and year are the associated values.

Now let's add some functionality to this dictionary.

In the text editor, below your existing code, write this code, save the file, and execute it:

```python
for name, details in birthdays.items():
    month = details["month"]
    year = details["year"]
    print(name + " was born in " + month + " " + str(year))
```

Wonderful work! You have now displayed each person's birthday in a more visually-appealing way. (By the way, you can delete the `print(birthdays)` line of code.)

Let's take this a step further and add some code that calculates how many years ago each person was born.

In the text editor, below your existing code, write this code, save the file, and execute it:

```python
maxine_birth_year = birthdays["Maxine"]["year"]
current_year = datetime.now().year
years_ago_maxine_born = current_year - maxine_birth_year
print("Maxine was born " + str(years_ago_maxine_born) + " years ago.")
```

We get an error! That's because we are attempting to use the *datetime* module but we haven't imported it yet. As the name states, the datetime module in Python provides tools to work with dates and times. Modules should be imported at the beginning of code files.

In the text editor, at the very top of your existing code, write this code, save the file, and execute it:

```python
from datetime import datetime
```

Awesome! Now it runs.

Here is the full code for reference:

```
from datetime import datetime
birthdays = {
    "Jack": {"month": "August", "year": 1985},
    "Emily": {"month": "March", "year": 1983},
    "Magnus": {"month": "March", "year": 2018},
    "Maxine": {"month": "July", "year": 1987},
    "Violet": {"month": "July", "year": 2008},
}
for name, details in birthdays.items():
    month = details["month"]
    year = details["year"]
    print(name + " was born in " + month + " " + str(year))
maxine_birth_year = birthdays["Maxine"]["year"]
current_year = datetime.now().year
years_ago_maxine_born = current_year - maxine_birth_year
print("Maxine was born " + str(years_ago_maxine_born) + " years ago.")
```

PARAMETERS AND ARGUMENTS

A *subprogram* is a reusable, self-contained block of code within a larger program that performs a specific task, often called a function, procedure, or method, which can be invoked (executed; activated) multiple times from different parts of the program to enhance maintainability and efficiency.

You might have a subprogram that adds two numbers. It could look like this:

```
def AddTwo(x, y):
    return x + y
```

Here, the name of the subprogram is "AddTwo".

Parameters are variables listed in a function's definition that allow you to pass values into the function for processing. "Passing values" refers to providing specific information to a function so it can use that information to complete its task.

In our above example subprogram, the parameters are the two numbers (x and y). The subprogram will return the sum of those two numbers.

The creation of a subprogram, as shown above, is called *defining* the subprogram. The above is an example of a subprogram definition.

Let's look at how that would be used in a main program. Say you had a school with two Physical Education classes per day, and you wanted to have the program calculate the total number of students in those classes. You could make a main program that made use of our "AddTwo" subprogram. It might look like this:

```
classSizePE1 = 25
classSizePE2 = 43
def AddTwo(x, y):
      return x + y
totalSize = AddTwo(classSizePE1, classSizePE2)
print("The total number of students in the PE classes is:", totalSize)
```

Let's look at this program line by line:

Line 1 and 2: The main program created two variables called classSizePE1 and classSizePE2, and gave each the value of 25 and 43, respectively.

Line 3 and 4: This line defines a subprogram called AddTwo that takes in two numbers (x and y) and returns their sum.

Line 5: Here, several key steps occur:
1) The main program created a variable called totalSize.
2) The main program called the subprogram AddTwo, providing it with the values of classSizePE1 and classSizePE2 (25 and 43).
3) Inside the subprogram AddTwo, these values were added together (resulting in 68).
4) The subprogram then returned this result (68) back to the main program.
5) The main program assigned this returned value to totalSize.

Line 6: The main program used the value stored in totalSize to display a message on the screen:

```
The total number of students in the PE classes is: 68.
```

This brings us to the concept of *arguments*. Arguments are the actual data passed to a subprogram when it is called. In the earlier example, the arguments are the numbers 25 and 43.

This comes from mathematics. In mathematics, there are formulas. These are exact math operations that are done in an exact order.

Typically, these math formulas need to be given some initial values to start processing the math steps. Those initial values are called arguments.

A subprogram doesn't necessarily need any arguments. Some subprograms may take one argument; some may take more than one.

To clarify: when a subprogram is defined, any data items it will need are called parameters. When the subprogram is actually used, any data passed to it at that time is called an argument.

Let's create a program that contains a subprogram, parameters, and arguments.

Write this code in the text editor, save the file, and run it:

```
def calculate_discounted_price(price, discount_rate):
    discount = price * discount_rate
    final_price = price - discount
    return final_price
item_price = float(input("Enter the original price of the item: $"))
discount_rate = 0.15
final_price = calculate_discounted_price(item_price, discount_rate)
print("Original price: $", item_price)
print("Discount rate:", int(discount_rate * 100), "%")
print("Final price after discount: $", round(final_price, 2))
```

This program defines a function, calculate_discounted_price, which takes price and discount_rate as inputs, calculates the discount by multiplying them, subtracts this discount from the price to get the final price, and returns it. In the main program, the user is prompted to enter the original item price, which is then converted to a decimal and stored in item_price. A fixed discount_rate of 0.15 is set, representing a 15% discount. The function is called with item_price and discount_rate, and the returned value is stored in final_price. Finally, the original price, the discount rate as a percentage, and the final price after discount (rounded to two decimal places) are printed.

So, what is the subprogram, parameters and arguments in this program?

• Subprogram (a self-contained, reusable section of code designed to perform a specific task): calculate_discounted_price is the subprogram that performs the discount calculation.

- Parameters (variables defined in a piece of code that determine what types of inputs the code can accept): `price` and `discount_rate` are the parameters defined in `calculate_discounted_price`, representing the expected inputs.

- Arguments (the actual values provided to a piece of code when it is executed): `item_price` and the fixed `discount_rate` value (0.15) are the specific arguments passed to `calculate_discounted_price` when it is called.

END OF CHAPTER CHALLENGE

Perform these actions:

1. Write a while loop that keeps doubling a number until it is over 100.

2. Write a for loop that prints out each individual letter of a word.

3. Create a dictionary with five keys, assign at least two values to each key, and display one item (such as the third item in the dictionary).

4. Write a program that includes: a subprogram, parameters, and arguments.

CHAPTER 7
BUILT-IN FUNCTIONS

As you have already seen in this book, Python comes with many functions that are built into the language. Let's learn some more of these!

STRING FUNCTION

The *string function (str())* converts any given value into a string (a sequence of characters), allowing it to be used or displayed as text. Without it, an error will occur if you try to combine non-string data (like numbers) with strings in print statements or other text-based outputs.

Write this code in the text editor, save the file, and run it:

```python
age = int(input("Enter your age: "))
if age < 2:
    category = "a baby"
elif age < 4:
    category = "a toddler"
elif age < 13:
    category = "a kid"
elif age < 20:
    category = "a teenager"
elif age < 65:
    category = "an adult"
else:
    category = "a senior citizen"
print("You are " + str(age) + " years old and you are " + category + ".")
```

Nicely done! Using the string function allowed us to display a number (the inputted age) along with a string in the print statement.

FLOAT FUNCTION

The *float function (float())* converts a number or a string that represents a number into a decimal (floating-point) value, making it possible to work with fractions and decimal places.

The float() function is useful because it allows precise calculations with decimal numbers, which is essential for tasks like financial calculations or scientific measurements. Without it, numbers would default to whole numbers (integers), potentially leading to inaccurate results when fractions are needed.

```
count = int(input("Enter how many numbers you want to average: "))
numbers = []
for i in range(count):
    num = float(input("Enter value " + str(i + 1) + ": "))
    numbers.append(num)
average = sum(numbers) / count
print("The average of your entered values is:", average)
```

Excellent work! In our program, the float() function converts each user input into a decimal format, allowing for accurate averaging of decimal values. Without it, inputs would default to integers, potentially losing any decimal precision and affecting the accuracy of the average calculation.

LENGTH FUNCTION

The *length function (len())* calculates and returns the number of items in a sequence (like a list, string, or tuple) or the number of keys in a dictionary.

Write this code in the text editor, save the file, and run it:

```
students = {
    "Mabel": "2nd",
    "Clyde": "3rd",
    "Ethel": "2nd",
    "Edgar": "4th",
    "Myrtle": "3rd",
    "Clarence": "2nd",
    "Hattie": "5th",
    "Wilbur": "4th",
    "Alma": "5th",
    "Otto": "3rd"
}
selected_grade = input(
    "Enter the grade (e.g., 2nd, 3rd, etc.) to display the number of students: "
)
students_in_grade = [
    student for student in students if students[student] == selected_grade
]
print("Number of students in", selected_grade + " grade:",
    len(students_in_grade))
```

Way to go! In our program, the len() function counts the number of students in the selected grade by returning the length of the students_in_grade list.

INTEGER FUNCTION

An *integer function (int())* converts a number, or a string that represents a whole number, into an integer.

Write this code in the text editor, save the file, and run it:

```
prices = []
num_items = int(input("Enter the number of items in your cart: "))
for i in range(num_items):
    price = float(input("Enter the price of item " + str(i + 1) + ": "))
    prices.append(price)
total_price = sum(prices)
print("The total price of the items in your cart is:", total_price)
```

Very good! In our program, the int() function converts the user's input for the number of items (num_items) into an integer, ensuring it is a whole number. If the user enters anything besides a whole number, they get an error.

ROUND FUNCTION

The *round function (round())* rounds a decimal (floating-point) number to a specified number of decimal places, or to the nearest whole number if no places are specified.

Write this code in the text editor, save the file, and run it:

```
principal = float(input("Enter the loan amount (principal): "))
annual_interest_rate = float(input("Enter the annual interest rate (as a percentage): "))
years = int(input("Enter the loan term in years: "))
monthly_interest_rate = (annual_interest_rate / 100) / 12
number_of_payments = years * 12
monthly_payment = principal * (
    (monthly_interest_rate * (1 + monthly_interest_rate) ** number_of_payments) /
    ((1 + monthly_interest_rate) ** number_of_payments - 1)
)
rounded_payment = round(monthly_payment, 2)
print("Your monthly loan payment is:", rounded_payment)
```

Excellent job! Here, we created a useful program to calculate monthly loan payments. The round() function in this program limits the monthly payment to two decimal places, making it useful for displaying a precise dollar amount that's easy to read and aligns with standard financial formatting.

SUM FUNCTION

The *sum function (sum())* adds up all the numbers in a collection (like a list) and returns the total.

Write this code in the text editor, save the file, and run it:

```
distances = []
for day in ["Monday", "Tuesday", "Wednesday", "Thursday", "Friday", "Saturday", "Sunday"]:
    distance = float(input("Enter distance covered on " + day + " (in miles): "))
    distances.append(distance)
total_distance = sum(distances)
print("Total distance covered in the week:", total_distance, "miles")
```

Good job! This program calculates how many miles the user traveled in a given week. The sum() function in this program adds up all the distances recorded for each day of the week, giving a total distance covered. This is useful because it provides a quick and accurate weekly total without needing to manually calculate each entry.

MAX AND MIN FUNCTIONS

The *maximum function (max())* finds and returns the largest value from a set of numbers or items in a collection, while the *minimum function (min())* finds and returns the smallest value from that same set. Together, these functions are useful for quickly identifying extremes within a collection.

Write this code in the text editor, save the file, and run it:

```
days = ["Monday", "Tuesday", "Wednesday", "Thursday", "Friday", "Saturday", "Sunday"]
temperatures = {}
for day in days:
    temp = float(input(f"Enter the temperature for {day}: "))
    temperatures[day] = temp
max_day = max(temperatures, key=temperatures.get)
min_day = min(temperatures, key=temperatures.get)
print("The highest temperature was on " + max_day + " at " + str(temperatures[max_day]) + " degrees.")
print("The lowest temperature was on " + min_day + " at " + str(temperatures[min_day]) + " degrees.")
```

Very good work! In this program, the max() function finds the highest temperature in the temperatures list, and min() finds the lowest temperature. These functions are useful because they quickly identify the temperature extremes for the week, allowing you to see the hottest and coldest days at a glance.

SORTED FUNCTION

The *sorted function (sorted())* returns a sorted version of a collection, like a list, without changing the original collection.

```
family_members = []
num_members = int(input("Enter the number of family members: "))
for i in range(num_members):
    name = input("Enter the name of family member " + str(i + 1) + ": ")
    family_members.append(name)
sorted_family = sorted(family_members)
print("Family members in alphabetical order:")
for member in sorted_family:
    print(member)
```

Wonderful job! We used the sorted function to display the names of our family members in alphabetical order.

END OF CHAPTER CHALLENGE

Perform these actions:

1. Write your own programs that utilize each of these built-in functions:
   a. String function (str())
   b. Float function (float())
   c. Length function (len())
   d. Integer function (int())
   e. Round function (round())
   f. Sum function (sum())
   g. Maximum function (max())
   h. Minimum function (min())
   i. Sorted function (sorted())

2. Research the type function – functiontype() – and create a simple program that utilizes it.

CHAPTER 8
MODULES

As a reminder, a *module* is a file containing Python code (such as functions, classes, or variables) that can be imported and reused in other programs.

The *os* module provides functions to interact with your operating system, such as reading and writing files, creating directories, and managing paths.

Write this code in the text editor, save the file, and run it:

```python
import os
desktop_path = os.path.join(os.path.expanduser("~"), "Desktop")
if not os.path.exists(desktop_path):
    desktop_path = os.path.join(os.path.expanduser("~"), "OneDrive", "Desktop")
grocery_list = {
    "Meat": ["Chicken", "Beef", "Pork"],
    "Dairy": ["Milk", "Cheese", "Yogurt"],
    "Produce": ["Apples", "Bananas", "Spinach"],
    "Bakery": ["Bread", "Bagels", "Muffins"],
    "Frozen": ["Frozen Vegetables", "Ice Cream"]
}
file_path = os.path.join(desktop_path, "grocery_list.txt")
with open(file_path, "w") as file:
    for category, items in grocery_list.items():
        file.write(category + ":\n")
        for item in items:
            file.write("  - " + item + "\n")
        file.write("\n")
print("Grocery list has been created on your Desktop at", file_path)
```

Wow! There's a lot happening here. Let's walk through this program line by line, defining the technical terms we've used in true Tech Academy style:

- `import os`: This line imports the os module, which (again) contains functions for interacting with the operating system (such as managing files).

- `desktop_path = os.path.join(os.path.expanduser("~"), "Desktop")`: This creates a path to the Desktop by getting the user's home directory with `os.path.expanduser("~")` and joining it with `"Desktop"` to specify the Desktop folder location.

- `if not os.path.exists(desktop_path):` This checks if the `desktop_path` directory actually exists on the computer. If it does not exist, the code inside the if statement will run.

- `desktop_path = os.path.join(os.path.expanduser("~"), "OneDrive", "Desktop")`: If the Desktop path was not found in the previous step, this line redefines `desktop_path` to look for it inside the OneDrive folder (a cloud storage service from Microsoft, where some users store their desktop).

- `grocery_list = { "Meat": ["Chicken", "Beef", "Pork"], ... }`: This defines a dictionary named `grocery_list`, where each key (like `"Meat"`) represents a category, and the values are lists of items in that category.

- `file_path = os.path.join(desktop_path, "grocery_list.txt")`: This creates a complete path for a new file named `grocery_list.txt` on the Desktop by joining `desktop_path` with the filename.

- `with open(file_path, "w") as file`: This opens `grocery_list.txt` in write mode (`"w"`), meaning it creates the file if it doesn't exist (or overwrites it if it does). The `with` statement ensures the file will automatically close after the program finishes writing to it. (As a note, a *with statement* is named for its structure of "with [context] as [variable]" and is used to manage resources like files, automatically handling setup and cleanup tasks [such as opening and closing files], ensuring they are properly closed after their use.)

- `for category, items in grocery_list.items()`: This loops through each category and its items in the `grocery_list` dictionary, where `category` is a section (like `"Meat"`) and `items` is the list of products in that section.

- `file.write(category + ":\n")`: This writes the category name followed by a newline (`"\n"`) to separate each category visually in the text file.

- `for item in items`: This loop goes through each individual item in the current category's list (like `"Chicken"` in `"Meat"`).

- `file.write(" - " + item + "\n")`: This writes each item to the file, preceded by a dash and some spaces for formatting, and adds a newline after each item.

- `file.write("\n")`: After finishing each category, this writes an additional newline to separate the categories in the file.

- `print("Grocery list has been created on your Desktop at", file_path)`: This prints a confirmation message, telling the user that the grocery list has been successfully saved to the specified file path on the Desktop.

CREATING MODULES

Did you know you can create your own module and use it? To do so, you write the module within a separate code file, and then import it into your main code file. Let's make and use our own module!

Complete these actions:

1. Create a new Python code file, and save it as greetings.py.

2. Within greetings.py, write and save this code:

```python
import datetime
def greet(name):
    current_hour = datetime.datetime.now().hour
    if current_hour < 12:
        time_of_day = "morning"
    elif current_hour < 18:
        time_of_day = "afternoon"
    else:
        time_of_day = "evening"
    greeting = "Good " + time_of_day + ", " + name + "! Welcome to the program."
    return greeting, time_of_day
def farewell(name, time_of_day):
    return "Goodbye, " + name + "! Have a great " + time_of_day + "!"
def ask_about_hobby(name):
    hobby = input("What is your favorite hobby, " + name + "? ")
    return "That's wonderful! Enjoy your time with " + hobby + "!"
```

3. Create another new Python code file, and save it as main.py.

4. Within main.py, write and save this code:

```python
import greetings
def main():
    while True:
        user_name = input("Enter your name (or type 'exit' to quit): ")
        if user_name.lower() == 'exit':
            print("Exiting the program. Goodbye!")
            break
        greeting_message, time_of_day = greetings.greet(user_name)
        print(greeting_message)
        hobby_message = greetings.ask_about_hobby(user_name)
        print(hobby_message)
        farewell_message = greetings.farewell(user_name, time_of_day)
        print(farewell_message)
        print()
if __name__ == "__main__":
    main()
```

Very well done! The module (greetings.py) defines functions to generate personalized greetings based on the time of day, provide farewell messages, and inquire about a user's favorite hobby, utilizing the current hour to tailor the interaction for a more engaging user experience. The main program (main.py) runs a loop that prompts the user for their name, displays a personalized greeting using the greet function, asks about their favorite hobby using the `ask_about_hobby` function, and concludes with a farewell message based on the time of day, allowing users to exit gracefully when desired.

TRY AND EXCEPT

Exceptions are events that occur during program execution that disrupt the normal flow of instructions (typically due to errors, such as invalid operations or unexpected inputs). "Raising" an exception means that the program has encountered a problem that it cannot handle, prompting it to signal that an error has occurred so it can be addressed appropriately. For example, ValueError is raised as an exception when a user inputs a letter instead of a requested number.

It is called an "exception" because it represents an event that deviates from the expected flow of execution in a program – showing that something unusual or unexpected has occurred.

The *try* and *except blocks* in Python are used for handling errors and exceptions. The code inside the try block is executed normally, but if an error occurs, the program jumps to the except block, allowing you to define how to respond to that error without crashing the program.

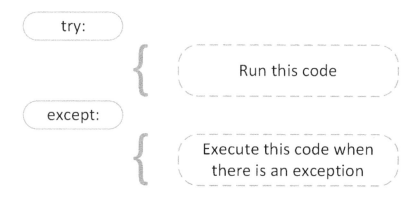

A real-world example of a try-except block is like a safety net for a tightrope walker: they attempt to cross the rope (the main task), but if they slip (an error occurs) the safety net (the except block) catches them and prevents a fall, allowing them to get back up and try again.

Write this code in the text editor, save the file, and run it:

```python
def calculate_average():
    numbers = []
    while True:
        try:
            user_input = input(
                "Enter a number to add to the list (or type 'done' to finish): "
            )
            if user_input.lower() == 'done':
                break
            number = float(user_input)
            numbers.append(number)
        except ValueError:
            print("Error: Invalid input. Please enter a numeric value.")

    if numbers:
        average = sum(numbers) / len(numbers)
        print("The average of the entered numbers is:", round(average, 2))
    else:
        print("No numbers were entered.")
if __name__ == "__main__":
    calculate_average()
```

Excellent work! This program prompts the user to enter a series of numbers to calculate their average, using try and except blocks to handle any invalid inputs (such as non-numeric values) by catching ValueError exceptions and prompting the user to enter valid numbers until they choose to finish.

END OF CHAPTER CHALLENGE

Perform these actions:

1. Create your own module, and import it into and use it within a different code file.

2. Write a program that utilizes the try and except blocks.

CHAPTER 9
OBJECT-ORIENTED PROGRAMMING

As we covered earlier, *objects* are items within computer programs that have both state and behavior. *Object-oriented* is an approach to programming that focuses on objects and data (as opposed to consecutive actions or some other approach).

You create objects by creating what are called *classes*. Classes are used to describe one or more objects. For example, we could create (or "declare") a class called a "Customer" class.

It is important to know that when you first create this class, you are describing the POTENTIAL characteristics and behavior of that TYPE of thing. You will still need to create an actual one of those things. That process is called "creating an INSTANCE" of the class, where "instance" means "an actual one" of the things described when you declared the class. When you do this, the data that makes up the object is kept in the computer's memory.

Instantiated refers to the process of creating a specific instance of an object from a class. Here is a diagram showing a car class with its instantiated objects:

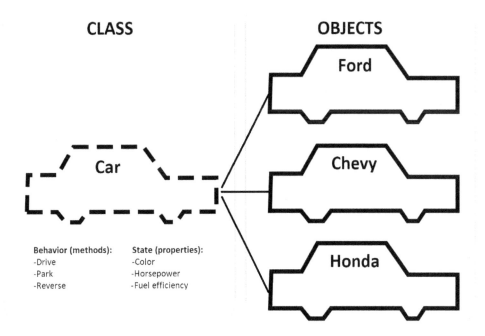

Let's look at another example. In a computer program designed to track pay records for all employees, you could have a class called "Employee".

Each program element representing an actual employee (Emily, Jack, Cherie, etc.) would be an instance of the "Employee" class. You would have one instance for each employee you entered into the computer.

Each time you created an "Employee" object, the computer would first find the "Employee" class, then use the definition of that class in creating that particular "Employee" instance using the data for the actual employee.

Consider this diagram, which shows a customer class and its associated objects:

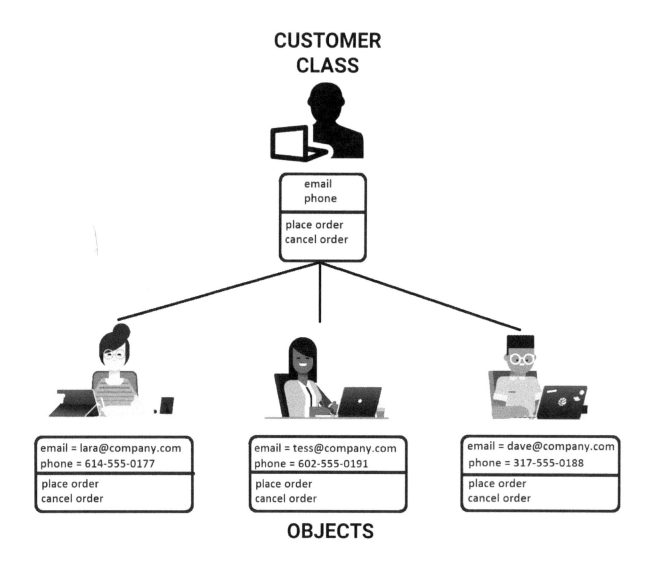

A *constructor* is a special part of a class (a template for defining an object). The constructor describes the default state of any new instance of the class that gets created. In other words, it gives default values for the properties of the class.

For example, let's look at a "Customer" class. The computer code to create the "Customer" class might look something like this:

```
class Customer
{
    string FullName;
    Boolean Active;
}
```

Now, let's say that whenever you created a new instance of the "Customer" class, you wanted it to be an active customer – in other words, you wanted the property "Active" to be set to "true".

To do this, you would make a constructor for the "Customer" class. It would be a small subprogram (function) inside the class that would be used every time an instance of the "Customer" class was created.

The constructor might look something like this:

```
Customer(string name) {
    FullName = name;
    Active = true;
}
```

The entire class would look like this:

```
class Customer
    {
    string FullName;
    Boolean Active;
    Customer(string name){
        Fullname = name;
        Active = true;
    }
}
```

The constructor would be used by asking for an instance of the "Customer" class to be created and passing along the desired name of the customer. The call (the act of execution) to create the instance of the class would look like this:

```
Customer cust = new Customer("Brenda Smith");
```

This creates a new instance of the "Customer" class using the constructor inside the class. The constructor uses the string "Brenda Smith" that it was given to set the value of the property "FullName" and uses the instruction in the constructor to set the property "Active" to "true."

The new instance of the "Customer" class, which is the variable "cust" here, will, therefore, have the properties:

```
FullName = "Brenda Smith";
Active = true;
```

(Note: The above code is given as an example and is not meant to be executed. We will create a constructor soon.)

In Python, a constructor is a special method called __init__ that you define inside a class. This method runs automatically whenever you create a new object from that class, and it is used to set up the object's properties. It is called __init__ because it is short for "initialize", indicating that this method is responsible for initializing (assigning; setting up) an object's attributes when it is created.

Write this code in the text editor, save the file, and run it:

```python
class Customer:
    def __init__(self, full_name, active=True):
        self.full_name = full_name
        self.active = active
    def display_info(self):
        status = "Active" if self.active else "Inactive"
        print("Customer Name:", self.full_name)
        print("Status:", status)
customer1 = Customer("Frodo Baggins")
customer2 = Customer("Gandalf the Grey", active=False)
customer3 = Customer("Aragorn II Elessar")
print("Customer Information:")
print("--------------------")
customer1.display_info()
print()
customer2.display_info()
print()
customer3.display_info()
```

Very good job! We used some of the fundamentals of object-oriented programming here. In fact, Python is an object-oriented programming language.

This program defines a Customer class that combines the attributes and behavior of a customer (specifically their full name and active status) utilizing a constructor (__init__) to initialize these properties. By creating instances of the Customer class ("Frodo Baggins", "Gandalf the Grey" and "Aragorn II Elessar") the program demonstrates object-oriented programming concepts such as organizing data (state) and methods (behavior) together within a single unit (the object).

AN OOP PROGRAM

To reinforce these important concepts, let's write another object-oriented program.

Write this code in the text editor, save the file, and run it:

```python
class BankAccount:
    def __init__(self, account_holder, balance=0.0):
        self.account_holder = account_holder
        self.balance = balance
    def deposit(self, amount):
        self.balance += amount if amount > 0 else 0
    def withdraw(self, amount):
        self.balance -= amount if 0 < amount <= self.balance else 0
    def display_balance(self):
        print(self.account_holder, "has a balance of:", self.balance)
account = BankAccount("Jack Bauer", 1000000)
account.deposit(50000)
account.withdraw(250000)
account.display_balance()
```

Excellent work! This program demonstrates object-oriented programming concepts by defining a BankAccount class that includes the state (attributes like account_holder and balance) and behaviors (methods such as deposit, withdraw, and display_balance) of a bank account. When an instance of the BankAccount class is created using the constructor (__init__), which initializes the object's attributes, illustrating the process of instantiation.

END OF CHAPTER CHALLENGE

Create a Book class that includes attributes for the title, author, and number of pages, and implements methods to display book information and check if the book is a novel (i.e., more than 100 pages).

CHAPTER 10
ROCK, PAPER, SCISSORS GAME

Now, using what you learned so far in this book, we will create rock, paper, scissors in Python! To start, create a new file in the code editor and save it as rock_paper_scissors.py on your desktop.

Within rock_paper_scissors.py, write, save, and execute this code:

```python
import random
def get_computer_choice():
    choices = ["rock", "paper", "scissors"]
    return random.choice(choices)
def get_user_choice():
    choice = input("Enter your choice (rock, paper, or scissors): ").lower()
    while choice not in ["rock", "paper", "scissors"]:
        print("Invalid choice. Please try again.")
        choice = input("Enter your choice (rock, paper, or scissors): ").lower()
    return choice
def determine_winner(user, computer):
    if user == computer:
        return "It's a tie!"
    elif (user == "rock" and computer == "scissors") or \
        (user == "scissors" and computer == "paper") or \
        (user == "paper" and computer == "rock"):
        return user.capitalize() + " beats " + computer + "! You win!"
    else:
        return computer.capitalize() + " beats " + user + "! Computer wins!"
def play_game():
    while True:
        user_choice = get_user_choice()
        computer_choice = get_computer_choice()

        print("You chose:", user_choice)
        print("Computer chose:", computer_choice)

        result = determine_winner(user_choice, computer_choice)
        print(result)
play_game()
```

Very well done! Go ahead and play the game a few turns.

This program uses concepts you learned in this book!

END OF CHAPTER CHALLENGE

Perform these actions:

1. Make the game "Elephant, Cat, Mouse" instead! Meaning, change "rock" to "elephant", "paper" to "mouse", and "scissors" to "cat".

2. Modify the game to keep score, displaying the number of games won by the user and the computer after each round.

3. Add functionality to allow the user to enter "exit" at any time to end the game.

CHAPTER 11
HANGMAN GAME

Let's build the classic game "Hangman" using Python! Start by creating a new file in the code editor and save it as hangman.py on your desktop.

Within hangman.py, write, save, and execute this code:

```python
Name = input('Please enter the name of the person who created this game: ')
print('This game was made by the amazing ' + Name + '!')
print('Welcome to my guessing game!')
print('In this program, you will try to guess a word that I chose.')
print('Good luck!')

def start():
    Player_Name = input('What is the name of the player? ')
    print('Greetings, ' + Player_Name + '! It is time to guess!')
    Secret_Word = 'Ostrich'.lower()
    Guesses = ''
    Turns_Left = 11
    while Turns_Left > 0:
        Wrong_Answers = 0
        for Letter in Secret_Word:
            if Letter in Guesses:
                print(Letter)
            else:
                print('_')
                Wrong_Answers += 1
        if Wrong_Answers == 0:
            print('YOU WIN! You guessed my word: ' + Secret_Word + '!!!!!')
            break
        Guess = input('Guess a letter here: ').lower()
        Guesses += Guess

        if Guess not in Secret_Word:
            Turns_Left -= 1
            print('Oops! This letter is not in my word. Please try again.')
            print('You have ' + str(Turns_Left) +
                    ' more guesses left. You can do it!')
            if Turns_Left == 0:
                print('GAME OVER.')

    def Play_Again():
        Again = input('Would you like to play the game again? ').lower()
        if Again == 'No'.lower():
            quit()
        if Again == 'Yes'.lower():
            start()
        else:
            print('Please enter Yes or No. Thank you!')
            Play_Again()
    Play_Again()

start()
```

(Note: You can find the full code at this link: bit.ly/techacademyfullpython.)

Awesome work! You should pick a word and then have a family member or friend play the game to try to guess it!

<u>END OF CHAPTER CHALLENGE</u>

`Change the number of guesses allowed in your program.`

It's time to create the game "Tic-Tac-Toe" using Python! Start by creating a new file in the code editor and save it as tic_tac_toe.py on your desktop.

Within tic_tac_toe.py, write, save, and execute this code:

```python
import random
import time
def print_board(b):
    print("   A   B   C")
    for i, row in enumerate(b):
        print(f"{i+1} {'|'.join(['_' + cell + '_' for cell in row])}")
def check_win(b, p):
    return (
        any(all(cell == p for cell in row) for row in b) or
        any(all(b[i][j] == p for i in range(3)) for j in range(3)) or
        all(b[i][i] == p for i in range(3)) or
        all(b[i][2 - i] == p for i in range(3))
    )
def get_computer_move(b):
    empty = [
        (i, j) for i in range(3)
        for j in range(3)
        if b[i][j] == ' '
    ]
    return random.choice(empty) if empty else None
def get_user_input(b):
    while True:
        try:
            user_input = (
                input("Enter your move (e.g., A1, B3): ")
                .upper()
                .replace(" ", "")
                .replace(",", "")
            )
            if (
                len(user_input) != 2 or
                user_input[0] not in "ABC" or
                user_input[1] not in "123"
            ):
                raise ValueError
            row = int(user_input[1]) - 1
            col = ord(user_input[0]) - ord('A')
            if b[row][col] != ' ':
                raise ValueError
            return row, col
```

(continued on the next page)

+

```python
        except ValueError:
            print("Invalid move. Try again.")
def is_board_full(b):
    return all(
        cell != ' '
        for row in b
        for cell in row
    )
def get_replay_input():
    while True:
        replay = input("Play again? (yes/y or no/n): ").lower()
        if replay in ['yes', 'y']:
            return True
        elif replay in ['no', 'n']:
            return False
        else:
            print("Invalid response. Please answer 'yes/y' or 'no/n'.")
def tic_tac_toe():
    while True:
        board = [[' ' for _ in range(3)] for _ in range(3)]
        print("Starting new game!")
        print_board(board)
        while True:
            row, col = get_user_input(board)
            board[row][col] = 'x'
            print("Player's move...")
            print_board(board)
            if check_win(board, 'x'):
                print("You win!")
                break
            elif is_board_full(board):
                print("It's a tie!")
                break
            print("Computer's move...")
            time.sleep(1)
            comp_row, comp_col = get_computer_move(board)
            if comp_row is not None:
                board[comp_row][comp_col] = 'o'
                if check_win(board, 'o'):
                    print_board(board)
                    print("Computer wins!")
                    break
                elif is_board_full(board):
                    print_board(board)
                    print("It's a tie!")
                    break
```

(continued on the next page)

```
        else:
            print_board(board)
    if not get_replay_input():
        break
tic_tac_toe()
```

(Note: You can find the full code at this link: bit.ly/techacademytictactoe.)

Very good job! You created a program that allows a user to play tic-tac-toe against a computer.

END OF CHAPTER CHALLENGE

Alter the program so that the computer goes first.

CHAPTER 13
TEXT-BASED ADVENTURE

Have you ever played the text-based adventure game called "Zork"? Let's go ahead and build a similar game in Python! Start by creating a new file in the code editor and save it as adventure.py on your desktop.

Within adventure.py, write, save, and execute this code:

```python
import random

class AdventureGame:
    def __init__(self):
        self.steps = [
            {
                "description": "You find yourself in a mystical forest. A cliff looms to the left.",
                "options": [
                    ("Follow the path right", 2),
                    ("Investigate the glowing cave straight ahead", 1),
                    ("Walk off the cliff", 0)
                ]
            },
            {
                "description": "A magical lake blocks your path. A whirlpool swirls dangerously.",
                "options": [
                    ("Use a levitation spell to float across", 2),
                    ("Wait for a magical ferry", 1),
                    ("Swim into the whirlpool", 0)
                ]
            },
            {
                "description": "A wild bear confronts you, its eyes glowing red.",
                "options": [
                    ("Cast a calming spell", 2),
                    ("Offer it your enchanted food", 1),
                    ("Try to wrestle the bear", 0)
                ]
            },
            {
                "description": "You discover a hidden grove with a mystical tree bearing golden fruit.",
                "options": [
                    ("Eat a fruit to gain wisdom", 2),
                    ("Plant a seed from the fruit", 1),
                    ("Cut down the tree for wood", 0)
                ]
            },
            {
                "description": "A group of friendly sprites invites you to dance in a moonlit glade.",
                "options": [
                    ("Join their dance", 2),
                    ("Politely decline and continue on", 1),
                    ("Chase them away", 0)
                ]
            },
            {
```

(continued on the next page)

```python
        "description": "A bridge guarded by a riddle-speaking troll blocks your path.",
        "options": [
            ("Solve the troll's riddle", 2),
            ("Wait for the troll to leave", 1),
            ("Try to fight the troll", 0)
        ]
    },
    {
        "description": "You come across a wizard dueling with a shadowy figure.",
        "options": [
            ("Help the wizard", 2),
            ("Observe from a distance", 1),
            ("Join the shadowy figure", 0)
        ]
    },
    {
        "description": "A mystical phoenix offers you a ride to your destination.",
        "options": [
            ("Accept the ride", 2),
            ("Politely decline and walk", 1),
            ("Try to capture the phoenix", 0)
        ]
    },
    {
        "description": "You find an ancient book with pages that seem to write themselves.",
        "options": [
            ("Read the book", 2),
            ("Ignore the book", 1),
            ("Destroy the book", 0)
        ]
    },
    {
        "description": "The final gate is inscribed with ancient runes.",
        "options": [
            ("Decipher the runes to open the gate", 2),
            ("Find a hidden key in the bushes", 1),
            ("Try to smash through the gate", 0)
        ]
    }
]
self.current_step = 0
self.game_over = False
self.score = 0

def shuffle_options(self, step):
    random.shuffle(step["options"])

def play_step(self):
    step = self.steps[self.current_step]
    self.shuffle_options(step)

    print(step["description"])
    for i, (option, _) in enumerate(step["options"], 1):
        print(f"{i}. {option}")
```

(continued on the next page)

```python
        while True:
            try:
                choice = int(input("Choose an option (1, 2, or 3): "))
                if choice not in [1, 2, 3]:
                    raise ValueError
                break
            except ValueError:
                print("Invalid choice. Please enter 1, 2, or 3.")

        _, points = step["options"][choice - 1]
        if points > 0:
            self.score += points
            print("Wise choice, adventurer. Continuing on...\n")
            self.current_step += 1
            if self.current_step == len(self.steps):
                self.game_over = True
                self.end_game()
        else:
            self.score -= 2
            print("Oops! You died. Let's try that again.\n")

    def end_game(self):
        if self.score >= 15:
            print(
                "Congratulations! Your wisdom and bravery have led to the happiest of endings. "
                "You have restored balance to the kingdom and are celebrated as a hero. "
                "You sit down on your golden throne, for some well-deserved rest, and a wise wizard "
                "(who looks suspiciously like Erik Gross) appears and says, \n"
                "\"In Tech Academy's halls, wisdom waits, "
                "A coding bootcamp path to open gates. "
                "Enroll, embark on this grand journey, "
                "Where success blooms from tech's tree.\""
            )
        elif self.score < 5:
            print(
                "Your journey was difficult, and you rose from the dead many times! "
                "Yet your persistence is to be admired. A mysterious figure appears from the shadows. "
                "It's a wizard who looks eerily similar to Erik Gross. And he whispers to you: \n"
                "\"Perseverance is key in the realm of tech. "
                "In the halls of Tech Academy, secrets beckon. "
                "Continue your quest, for knowledge is the treasure on this trek. "
                "Enroll in a coding boot camp, it's the key to success I reckon.\""
            )
        else:
            print(
                "You've completed your journey. Though not every decision was perfect, "
                "you've done well and earned the respect of others. An old wizard "
                "(who looks suspiciously like Erik Gross) suddenly appears, and tells you, \n"
                "\"In Tech Academy's realm of lore, "
                "Coding bootcamps unlock the door. "
                "Join this quest, in wisdom steep, "
                "For success in life, rewards to reap.\""
            )

    def start_game(self):
        while not self.game_over:
            self.play_step()

if __name__ == "__main__":
    game = AdventureGame()
    game.start_game()
```

Note: You can find the full code at this link: bit.ly/adventure_python (include an underscore between "adventure" and "python").

Phenomenal work!

<u>END OF CHAPTER CHALLENGE</u>

Add your own multiple choice adventure options and customize the journey!

CHAPTER 14
FINAL CHALLENGES

For the final assignments in this book, we are providing you with a series of challenges to complete. You can perform these tasks by applying the data you learned in this book – yet, some will also require online research. Simply put, these challenges include tasks you have not previously learned to do, and they are an excellent opportunity for self-teaching and debugging!

```
Complete these actions:
```

1. Build a program that simulates a coin flip and prints whether it lands on heads or tails.

2. Write a program that asks the user to input a number and then prints out whether it's even or odd.

3. Write a program that takes an integer and prints whether it is positive, negative, or zero.

4. Create a function that asks the user for their name and then prints it in reverse.

5. Create a function that asks for a user's name and prints it in all uppercase letters.

6. Write a program that uses the range() function to print all even numbers from 0 to 20.

7. Create a program that uses range() to print numbers from 10 down to 1 in reverse.

8. Write a program that asks for a number and checks if it's within the range of 1 to 100.

9. Write a program that takes a sentence from the user and counts the number of vowels.

10. Build a function that accepts two numbers and prints all numbers between them using the range() function.

11. Build a program that asks for the user's height in inches and converts it to feet and inches.

12. Create a program that converts a given number of days into weeks, hours, minutes, and seconds.

13. Write a program that takes a user's birthdate and calculates their age in years and months.

CONGRATULATIONS!

You have reached the end of our book! Well done for your hard work and persistence!

You should now have a basic understanding of Python and coding. We have successfully laid a firm foundation on which to build upon. Now that you have these basics in place, you can excel your skills to build more advanced websites and software.

To accomplish taking your skill set to the next level, read the next book in this series! In it, we will teach you new tools and how to build stronger programs.

Thank you for your time and attention, and good luck!

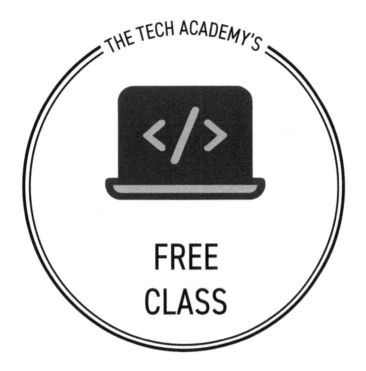

Want to learn the basics of computer programming in a few hours?

Enroll in an online, *free* Intro to Coding Class from The Tech Academy now!

These classes were designed for absolute beginners.

All important terms and concepts are defined at the beginning of each class and no previous knowledge or experience is required.

We have free classes for kids and adults!

Try out coding and enroll in a free online coding class today!

learncodinganywhere.com/freeclass

OTHER READING

Be sure to check out other Tech Academy books, which are all available for purchase on Amazon:

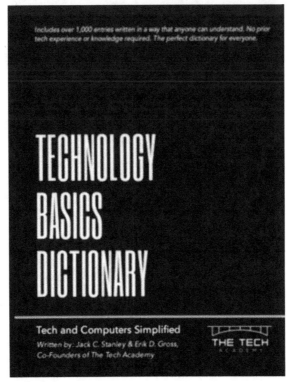

PROJECT MANAGEMENT

HANDBOOK

Simplified Agile, Scrum and DevOps for Beginners

Written by
Jack C. Stanley & Erik D. Gross
Co-Founders of The Tech Academy